MEXICAN MONUMENTS

MEXICAN MONUMENTS

strange encounters

Conceived and Coordinated by Helen Escobedo
With Photographs by Paolo Gori
And Essays by Nestor García Canclini, Rita Eder,
Fernando González Gortázar, Jorge Ibargüengoitia,
Jorge Alberto Manrique, and Carlos Monsivais

Abbeville Press · Publishers · New York

Editor: Walton Rawls
Designers: Paolo Gori and Molly Shields
Production Supervisor: Hope Koturo
Translator: Elena C. Murray

Library of Congress Cataloging-in-Publication Data

Mexican monuments : strange encounters / [edited by] Helen
  Escobedo and Paolo Gori.
      p.   cm.
    ISBN 0-89659-906-X
      1. Monuments—Mexico. 2. Memorials—Mexico.   I. Escobedo,
      Helen.   II. Gori, Paolo.
    NA9348.M6M46   1989
    730′ .972—dc19   88-36694
                                                        CIP

"The Eloquence of Stone" by Jorge Ibargüengoitia originally appeared in
Excelsior, a leading Mexican newspaper, where the author was a regular
columnist. The article was anthologized in *Viajes en la America Ignota* (Joaquin
Mortiz, Mexico, 1972).

CONTENTS

The Monument to the Free Textbook, in Tijuana, Baja California, is graphically precise: a huge, open book (with the words ''I can'' on its cover) standing against the backdrop of the national flag at the top of a flight of stairs, with ever-hopeful children striving toward it.

FOREWORD
Helen Escobedo

The photographs and essays presented in this book are the result of a long collaborative effort with Paolo Gori that began in 1980. During that year, as a fellow of the department of humanities and a founding member of the short-lived Laboratory for Research in Urban Art at the National University of Mexico, I set myself the task of developing an idea long toyed with. I wanted to publish an illustrated essay on urban sculpture with regard to placement in outdoor open spaces, validity as landmark or signal, as definer of place, and as focal point for pedestrian and vehicular traffic.

Being a site-oriented sculptor myself, I suddenly became aware of the obvious fact that whereas nearly all civic monuments are superbly sited, public sculpture seldom is, and it was at that point I began reflecting on a series of questions: What is the difference between a sculpture and a monument? What distinguishes an urban sculpture from a civic monument?

Can a sculpture become a monument, and if so, when? Are all good sculptors capable of designing a monument?

I thought of the *Balzac* by Rodin, and I began to look carefully at new and vintage statuary. The questions and answers tumbled about me in such ever-widening circles that I knew if I did not circumscribe my thoughts I would have three essays going instead of one. In any case I was increasingly fascinated by the wealth of national iconography so evident in civic monuments in and around Mexico City; I found that what I began to need badly was an excellent photographer who shared my enthusiasm in seeking out promising monuments. And that is how it all began, an eight-year odyssey that was to take me and Paolo on a thorough exploration of the entire country. We followed our noses like pigs to truffles and unearthed monuments that swung from the massive and sophisticated through the pretentious, vulgar, and obnoxious to the modest, funny, and often endearing creations of naïves, who produced the uninhibited examples of the bizarre and the vernacular that give this book its true enchantment.

Some generalizations come to mind when seeking answers in regard to differentiating between public sculpture and civic monuments and among those who design, model, or carve them, be they sculptors, technicians who specialize in enlarging scale models, or simple amateurs with flair; for to undertake the making of a monument rather than a work of art, an artist or master craftsman must conform to certain rules applicable to civic statuary commissioned by private or public bodies to honor the image of a person or an idea.

Among the mandates for civic monuments is the use of historically accepted symbols—for bravery: jaws set, hands clenched, arms raised as for battle; for justice: a standing or sitting lady blindfolded and holding a pair of scales and a sword; and for beauty: a girl-woman or a boy-man. For heroes with distinctive idiosyncracies, they should be much in evidence; Winston Churchill must sport a cigar or hold up two fingers in a V for victory. Kings, generals, and presidents must ride magnificent horses (whether horsemen or not), and warriors should be crowned with wreaths of laurel. Other commissions decree the use of large bases that add greater stature to the figures by raising them well above eye level—to create a sense of awe and respect in the ordinary mortals below.

The placement of civic statuary, usually superlative, was, and still is, at such a focal point as the entrance to a palace or a government building, in the center of a square, at the head of a mall, or in the middle of a traffic circle. When the work refers specifically to a site, such as, for instance, a waterfront or a promenade by the sea, it may be of a lesser scale but still must be in keeping with a theme, an ode to fishermen, mermaids, or perhaps a Triton, with a pronged instrument raised high.

Budgets for making monuments are generally far more generous than those for outdoor sculpture, particularly in developing countries where no matter how famous the artists are they will be lucky not to be out of pocket by the time their work is finally erected. On the other hand, those commissioned to execute commemorative pieces are well remunerated, indeed!

Another spin-off for monument makers, and very much in their favor, is the absence of problems provoking public hazard, solely due to perfect siting and obeisance to the laws of monumentality—meaning, out of reach.

With all such matters in mind, I began to look at the glut of monuments to see whether these rules really applied. I found to my glee that to those monuments that delighted and enchanted me most, they did not; needless to say, to the pompous predictable ones they nearly always did, with their overwhelming scale and their bourgeoisness, so rhetorical and authoritarian. But then there were the others (those that sent us far and wide throughout the republic seeking more), monuments made from an honest sense of need, with little or no money, made with emotion and feeling, without methodology, even at times without craft, but with immense spontaneity and originality.

No doubt you will find in the pages of this photographic adventure examples of some monuments that appear too awful, too achingly pathetic and poorly made to warrant their having been selected. Others may seem idiotic or even hilariously funny, but then blessed be those who had the daring to come up with such fresh ideas as a monument to the free textbook, the straw hat, the shrimp, the cricket, or the octopus. How short of money must you be to make a little hero 20 centimeters high and put him on a cement base 3 meters high and then paint him silver? How creative must local craftsmen be to make such different bases for assembly-line casts of national heroes that they look ideally sited because they reflect elements of the local architecture? Who on earth came up with the idea of a monument to the great sewage system? Who decides where to put these monuments, for freestanding, sitting, or lying recumbent, our frozen heroes abound, lost in the jungle of buildings, roadsides, and traffic jams, or towering above the pygmied pedestrian, who seldom, when asked, has a clue as to the giant's identity, or even whether he exists at all, either as a pleasing landmark or as a civic protuberance.

All this and much more will come to mind as you peruse these pages, going from shock to horror to mirth and enchantment, a litmus test for personal analysis regarding the meaning of sculpture versus monument, freedom versus reconciliation and commitment, harmony versus outrage. Why not cast a fresh look at all the effigies you have taken for granted within your own vicinity? Search for those others, the strange ones that may be there, or sadly, may not.

The sad remains of an attempted androgynous leap into space is to be found in Oteapán, a remote Indian village on the coast of Veracruz.

BY WAY OF INTRODUCTION
Fernando González Gortázar

Dear Helen:

It has been almost a year since we got together to admire the splendid photographs of your "Unusual Monuments." Despite the time that has passed and the haste with which, unfortunately, I had to look over the material, your "discoveries" keep turning over in my mind, provoking a few thoughts I would like to share with you. What struck me the most, as the days go by, is the "change of heart" I have had regarding these works. I recall that as we gazed at the photos (impeccable, I repeat), we laughed over them and sometimes even became indignant at the sight of those blunders, those grotesque images. There is no doubt in my mind that many of your "monuments" are preposterous and grotesque, laughable, extravagant, ridiculous, outlandish, un-

---

Fernando González Gortázar is an architect, sculptor, and artist. His particular field of interest is urban art.

sightly, misshapen, crude and the other nine words included in my *Great Dictionary of Synonyms*. But every time I think about them and compare those qualifiers to: flat, insipid, conventional, presumptuous, pedantic, tedious, unsubstantial, uprooted, hybrid, spurious, and a million etceteras that come to mind whenever I think of the small world around us and of the high percentage of art (whether public or not) that pollutes it, your monuments seem all the more valuable and important as a whole.

There are exceptions, of course; some pieces are positively distasteful because they have been manipulated or because they are purportedly manipulatory. But in a great number of them, in the bulk of your "finds," there is a great deal to be thankful for. What vitality in a country of disenchantment! What candor and freshness among so many hard-boiled scoundrels! What straightforwardness and what heterodoxy amid such pretense and such institutional loyalty!

I believe that there are more and more of us who wonder whether Mexico is merely a name confined between two borders or if it actually means something. For many people, perhaps for a great many, being a Mexican is a curse—hopefully transitory—until the advent of that glorious day of our definitive and hallowed Northamericanization. But Mexico does exist, and it is here, as a reality, a product of its history, its regions, its influences, its paradoxes, and its contradictions. Its national identity, ever-changing and diverse, cannot, of course, be demonstrated. It is nevertheless, I believe, demonstrated in one thing or another: in this landscape, in that subtle turn of phrase, in this work of art, in that culinary marvel, in so many, many things that for some reason and to a certain degree are Mexican. There were others in the past, as also there will be in the future. I believe, Helen, that among your "finds" there just might be some answers to our increasing loss of culture, and that somewhere there is a slender thread that binds us to something very profound and very valuable that I cannot quite define. If I'm right, then you have a veritable treasure.

And now, there is one more concern: the preservation of such a treasure. It disturbs me to think that its absurdity, its challenging absence of artifice and conventionality, its aggressive determination, and in some cases, its sheer ugliness, may turn this treasure into condemned prisoners on the way to the gallows. But these are my own private quirks. Perhaps the destiny of these works will be completely fulfilled when they contradict the pompous endurance of the "works of art" by proving that it is those small transitory gestures that, if coherent, fill the lives of peoples and of nations alike. In any case, your "discoveries" are in the world and in their avatars. Even if they should disappear, their lessons will still remain, there, in the photographs themselves.

13   This lady points out the entrance to a residential development in Cancún, Yucatán.

The central figure in a monument to the road builder on the Mexico City–Toluca highway.

15   David Alfaro Siqueiros as Prometheus on his tomb in the Panteón de Dolores, Mexico City. Sculpted by Alejandro Ortega, one of his pupils.

One way to dispose of obsolete aircraft, at the Presidential Hangar, in Mexico City's International Airport.

The aerodynamic rendering of this monument in the state of Coahuila suggests that President Lázaro Cárdenas could steer unblinkingly into the eye of any storm.

This gigantic head of President López Mateos overlooks the city of Toluca, State of Mexico.

Next to Mexico City's mammoth Hotel de México, a venture that nearly broke magnate Luis Suárez, stands Siqueiros's famed Polyforum (above), which was sponsored by Suárez as an attraction. On one visit, both artist and patron were standing; on a subsequent visit they were lying on the ground—such is life in the tropics.

21

To get to the lovely ruins of Palenque, one must overtake this somewhat unnerving version of classic
Mayan features.

23   Surging up out of the middle of the road, this figure marks the entrance to the town of Campeche. The
inscription on its base reads: "A determined people will accomplish the impossible."

In the town of Yanga, Veracruz, stands a monument to the legendary (and well endowed) ''King'' Yanga, leader of a band of runaway slaves. Behind him is a primitive sugarcane press.

El Pípila, the landmark of Guanajuato City, is the subject of much reflection on the part of Jorge
Ibargüengoitia in the following chapter. ▶

THE ELOQUENCE OF STONE
Jorge Ibargüengoitia

I might be accused of dealing with a select minority, but, so far, I have not met a single Mexican who entertains the hope, much less the desire, for his bones to wind up in the *Rotonda de los Hombres Ilustres*.[1] This observation has always perplexed me, because it is evident that our hero worship and the tendency to build monuments for heroes are two increasingly widespread phenomena that are transforming our cities and that emanate from, or at least should emanate from, a spirit of emulation.

The fact that one of the main industries in a country where nobody wants to be a hero is the construction of monuments to heroes requires a deeper investigation than I have been able to carry out, but for the time being I shall refer to concrete evidence. A few years ago in San Miguel Allende, a Spanish physician gave a lecture where he explained that since ancient

Jorge Ibargüengoitia, humorist, columnist, and writer, was killed in a plane crash in 1984.

Monument to Siqueiros, an ink drawing by Rogelio Naranjo, a well-known political cartoonist.

times this country has been inhabited by people who tended to embark upon huge, laborious constructions whose practical purpose was impossible to determine. His remarks were not only interesting and a little insulting but prophetic as well, since it is precisely in San Miguel Allende where a recently completed enterprise constitutes the perfect example of this tendency: the municipal market was demolished in order to build a statue of Allende.[2] Since the stalls and the vendors set up shop out in the street, obstructing the vehicular traffic, the rats now live and thrive in the private homes.

When I was a child and had spent long periods of time in Acapulco, I used to think that the city would be beautiful once it was completed, when one no longer had to leap around among mounds of gravel. Why? Because the buildings that had stood there then, the pride and joy of Mexican architecture, had crumbled with age, and, besides, they were erecting a monument to the Heroes along the waterfront.

This monument, by the way, has very interesting characteristics: a triangle resting on a stone base, with a bust on each one of its vertices. On the topmost point, a bust of Hidalgo, thrice larger than life, is depicted with a distinct grimace.[3] To his left (the spectator's right), the bust of Morelos, twice the normal size, is easily recognizable by the familiar kerchief tied around his head.[4] On the third vertex of the triangle is the bust of an anonymous, or, better said, unidentified personage, wearing an early nineteenth-century military uniform, who could well be Guerrero,[5] Allende, Iturbide,[6] or even Calleja,[7] for that matter.

28

Two important lessons may be derived from observing this monument: one for the sculptor and the other for the spectator who may happen to be an aspiring hero. The sculptor must understand that for the observer unacquainted with baroque art terminology, the differences in size among the three busts on the same monument does not necessarily mean there is a difference in the status of the personages represented, nor in the magnitude of their respective feats, but merely that there is a difference in the size of their heads, and that upon observing the monument it could be concluded that some of the famous men depicted here had extremely large heads while others were decidedly microcephalic. However, an even more interesting and perhaps even more profitable lesson offered by this monument to the would-be hero is this: if you aren't bald or not in the habit of winding a cloth around your head, you have to develop a trademark, like, for example, wearing square eyeglasses, growing a remarkable beard—whether it be very shaggy, spindly, or extremely long—or covering one eye with a patch, since no one really notices the face, and a hero without an image might as well not exist at all.

Right at the entrance to the city of Chilpancingo, there is a monument so unique it is truly extraordinary: a rectangular block of polished stone with no relief whatsoever, not even a plaque. I inquired to whom this monument was dedicated. No one could give me the answer. I kept wondering what a rectangular block of polished stone could possibly represent, until it finally dawned on me: it is a monument to

the rectangular monolith, or perhaps it is the very monolith itself.

Two

During Cárdenas's[8] time, a monument to El Pípila[9] was erected in Guanajuato. When it was finished, all of Guanajuato said that it was a monstrosity; it was ill-proportioned; El Pípila didn't look like that at all since he was a consumptive; and that if he was nicknamed Pípila it was because he had a turkey face, etc.[10] Who would ever have dreamed that in time El Pípila was to become Guanajuato's answer to the Eiffel Tower? Nevertheless, about thirty percent of the postcards sold in Guanajuato today bear the likeness of El Pípila.

It's quite possible that public indignation would have been far greater if, instead of a monument to El Pípila, it had been to Hidalgo. Somebody, of course, would be sure to protest against the construction of a monument to a personage whose birthplace in that state is uncorroborated, while someone else was sure to remark: "He was just an upstart who botched everything up."

El Pípila, it must be admitted, is the perfect hero. His origin is as obscure as his birthplace is certain. Since no one really knows his last name, there is no danger of his descendants clamoring for pensions. His role in History was brief, eloquent, and decisive; no famous last words. This last characteristic permitted the then governor of the state to insert one of his own phrases on the base of El Pípila's statue: "There are still some more *alhondigas* left to be burned," a phrase that, at the time, made all the landowners quake in their boots, and would be seriously considered by the censorship office should it appear in the dialogue of a film.

When the mines of Guanajuato dwindled down and were no longer the city's main industry, having been replaced by tourism, a monument to the miners was erected. As a result, one of the most delightful parks in town—and probably in the whole country—was completely ruined. The fountain in the center was removed and a pedestal built in its place. At that time it seemed original enough, but now after the Olympic Games it looks like either a poor imitation of a high diver's platform or, at best, its rudimentary predecessor. This pedestal supported the bronze image of a bare-chested, slightly hunchbacked Guanajuato miner wearing a helmet—the kind that is no longer worn. Clutched in his hands and leaning on his pelvis so that it seems to sprout from his trousers at a thirty-degree angle, there is an enormous compressed-air drill, tirelessly and perpetually flailing the void. The monument is topped off by a series of protuberances emerging from the park grounds that turn out to be carved, polished bronze busts, copied from passport-size photos of the personages whose names appear on the pedestals. The principal flaw in this part of the monument lies in the fact that nobody knows who these gentlemen were, since the names don't ring a bell; however, one might infer that these busts represent men who paid with their lives for the negligence and miserliness of some mining company.

Juárez on a Turtle, an old stamp, ink, and gouache by Francisco Toledo. One of a series dedicated to Benito Juárez.

Whenever I visit Guanajuato and see that monument, it occurs to me that in time, let's say a couple of centuries from now, once the tourist phase has passed, a monument to the hotel manager will be erected. I should like to take this opportunity to suggest that he be portrayed as wearing a cutaway coat, a carnation in his lapel, and presenting the bill.

Three

Just like the animal species that apparently seems to evolve according to the needs imposed on it by the environment, monuments, too, undergo an evolution according to the needs of the governments that have them built. A case in point is the most important monument still left from the Colonial period: the equestrian statue of a king who probably never was a good horseman, who never dressed up as a Roman except perhaps to have breakfast or to attend a costume ball, and whose exploits, as far as anyone can recall, were nothing but a series of abominations. But he was a king and that was that. They built him his statue, which now goes by the name of *El Caballito*.[11] Porfirio Díaz's government was devoted to digging up heroes, some famous, some unknown, and representing them in the realistic manner at the peak of their heroic careers.[12] For example, Columbus, holding in one hand plans of the world as he conceived it and shading his forehead with the other, his gaze fixed on the horizon, is probably exclaiming "America!" to himself while spotting a dark line—or perhaps, unaware of the grave injustice that would be done him, "Columbia!"

Father Hidalgo, brandishing a banner and ignoring the golden angel over his head (shamelessly stealing the show), is undoubtedly saying what they said he said that day, "Long live Mexico! Long live Fernando VII! Death to the Gachupines!"[13]

The heroes of our unfortunate wars are portrayed, or should be portrayed, as hurtling into space shrouded in the flag or grasping a broken, though unsheathed, sword and saying to the invader, "if we only had ammo!"

With the Revolutionary governments, there is a new trend in Mexican monuments that consists of continuous attempts to represent abstract ideas in a figurative manner.[14] For example, a shirtless man wiping his brow with one hand and holding a useless sledgehammer in the other represents Labor. (And speaking of metaphors, the absence of a shirt could well mean not only Labor but, rather, poorly remunerated labor at that.)

A woman holding her child in her arms represents yet another abstract idea: Mother. At the foot of the Monument to the Mother, there is an inscription, in gold letters, that reads, "To the one who gave us her love even before knowing us." Can you ask for anything more abstract than that? Incidentally, this phrase always seemed incomplete to me. It should say, "To the one who, in some cases, gave us her love even before knowing us and who, in general, after knowing us, spoiled us rotten." Thus, the sentence is slightly longer, but considerably more accurate, I believe.

Social Security is another concept that has been represented in the realistic manner as follows: A woman, obviously a mother, totally engrossed in contemplating the child in her arms who is obviously her son, is unaware that behind her, an enormous bird—an eagle according to some, a roc according to others—is getting ready to devour her, offspring and all.[15]

Recently, there has been a new trend in monuments as a result of the Olympic Games and as a sign that Mexico is now a full-fledged member of the International Community. It consists in depicting abstract ideas by means of abstract forms; that is, they don't really represent anything, but...(listen closely now, because this is very important) some inscriptions are added that apparently give the name of a street but, in fact, express the abstract idea it strives to represent. For example, no one would ever realize that the monuments on the *Ruta de la Amistad* (Friendship Route) have anything at all to do with friendship if the avenue had not been so named. But that's what it's called, and consequently those monuments are monuments to friendship. At present there is a new tendency toward even greater abstractionism. It is quite likely that in the future there won't even be any monuments at all, but rather that the buildings themselves will be so expressive that one glance will be enough to perceive the aspirations of a nation. There is a remarkable example of this in the metro stations, which express the expectations of all us Mexicans aspiring to better and richer lives. The entrance, paradoxically, leads downward to the bowels of the earth, where the passing trains will smoothly and efficiently transport you to the slums of Balbuena.

Translator's Footnotes

1. *La Rotonda de los Hombres Ilustres*, roughly translated as the Monument to Distinguished Men, is located in the San Fernando Cemetery in Mexico City's Guerrero district. Famous statesmen, artists, diplomats, et al., are buried there.

2. Ignacio Allende (1779–1811), one of the principal leaders of Mexico's independence from Spain, was shot the year after the revolt began.

3. Miguel Hidalgo y Costilla (1753–1811) was a parish priest in the town of Dolores. It was Father Hidalgo who led the armed revolt against the Spaniards. On the 16th of September, 1810, he proclaimed the rebellion by ringing his church bell and calling the people to arms. He managed to lead his ragged army to several victories, and took several cities, including Guanajuato. Hidalgo was eventually captured and executed in Chihuahua.

4. Jose María Morelos y Pavón (1765–1815), also a priest like Hidalgo, is considered another great hero of the Independence. Morelos waged several successful military campaigns and gathered together the first National Congress in Chilpancingo in 1813. He was defeated by Agustín de Iturbide, taken prisoner, and shot. Morelos was said to have suffered from migraine headaches, which he attempted to relieve by tying a kerchief around his head; hence he is always easily identified.

5. Vicente Guerrero (1793–1824) also fought in the War of Independence and became president of the Republic in 1829. He was overthrown by a coup d'etat and shot in Oaxaca.

6. Agustín de Iturbide (1783–1824). Unlike Hidalgo, Morelos, Allende, Aldama, and Guerrero, who are undisputed heroes of Mexico's Independence, Iturbide is a highly

controversial figure even today. Although he first served with the viceroy's army, he then joined forces with Guerrero's army and was instrumental in obtaining recognition of the Independence from the then viceroy O'Donoju. In 1822 he was crowned emperor, but was forced to abdicate the following year, since this act was regarded as a betrayal of the Republic's ideals. He fled to Italy, but was shot upon his return to Mexico. Needless to say, Ibarguengoitia's remark that this unidentified figure might well be Iturbide or even Calleja is obviously a joke.

7. Felix María Calleja del Rey (1759–1828) was a Spanish general who fought against Hidalgo, defeating him in 1811. Calleja was viceroy from 1813 to 1816.

8. Lázaro Cárdenas (1895–1970) was president of Mexico from 1934 to 1940. He is best remembered for having nationalized the oil industry in 1938 and for promoting agrarian reform and opening Mexico's doors to a host of Spanish refugees during the Spanish Civil War.

9. El Pípila is one of the great popular heroes of the Mexican Independence. Contrary to what Ibargüengoitia mentions, his last name has been fairly well established: Juan José de los Reyes Martinez. During the capture of Guanajuato, 800 men (miners, convicts, Indians, etc.) led by Hidalgo stormed a large warehouse where grain was stored and where the Spaniards, led by Lieutenant Riano, had held their ground. El Pípila, a poor Indian, is remembered for his feat of courage and strength: on September 28, 1810, he tied a rock on his back for protection and battered down the door of the Alhondiga while his companions burned it down.

10. Pípila, in the vernacular of the time, meant "female turkey."

11. The statue is of Carlos IV of Spain, popularly known as *El Caballito* (The Little Horse) and a well-known landmark in Mexico City since it was erected in 1803. Although it has been changed from place to place throughout the years, it is now located in front of the National Museum of Art, on Tacuba Street in downtown Mexico City.

12. Porfirio Díaz (1830–1915) played a vital part as a military man during the French Intervention (1861–67) in support of Juárez's government, which he later rebelled against. Díaz was president of Mexico several times: first in 1876, then from 1877 to 1880, and finally from 1884 to 1911. His administration gradually became a dictatorship that provoked the Mexican Revolution of 1910 and also acquired a name: *El Porfiriato*. He was overthrown by Francisco I. Madero and was exiled to France where he died in 1915.

13. *Gachupines* is a derogatory term for Spaniards.

14. Ibargüengoitia is probably referring to the post-Cárdenas politicians who refer to the Revolution as a matter of course in order to support their policies, whatever they may be.

15. A roc was a huge white bird in *The Arabian Nights*.

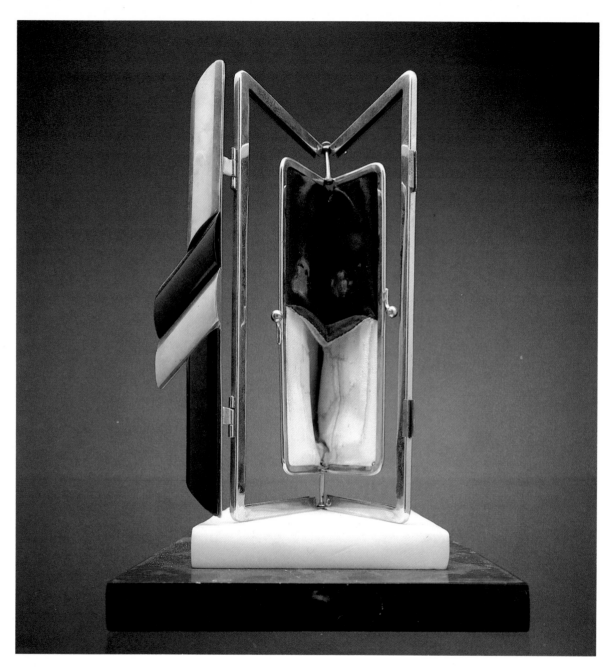

Monument to "La Bourse" (meaning the Stock Exchange), a leather and metal purse found in the Lagunilla flea market by Alan Glass, a Canadian artist residing in Mexico City.

34

A Letter

Dear Helen:

I extend a monumental apology for having failed to write an article on monuments, but I confess that it is a topic of such gigantic proportions that entire volumes would be needed for this undertaking. Just imagine, for instance, all the trials and tribulations undergone by *El Caballito, The Angel, Columbus* (who was stashed away for two years in the railroad station until it was finally placed where it belongs), "The Green Indians," the calamities that befell Enrico Martinez, the misadventures of Agustín Querol's *Pegasus,* etc., etc.

From this dubious Cuernavaca, plagued with statues, some of them deplorable, others horrid, all of them unusual, I send you a strong bronzelike hug, patina and all.

Pedro Friedeberg

Pedro Friedeberg is a surrealist painter, sculptor, and creator of unusual objects. He lives in San Miguel Allende.

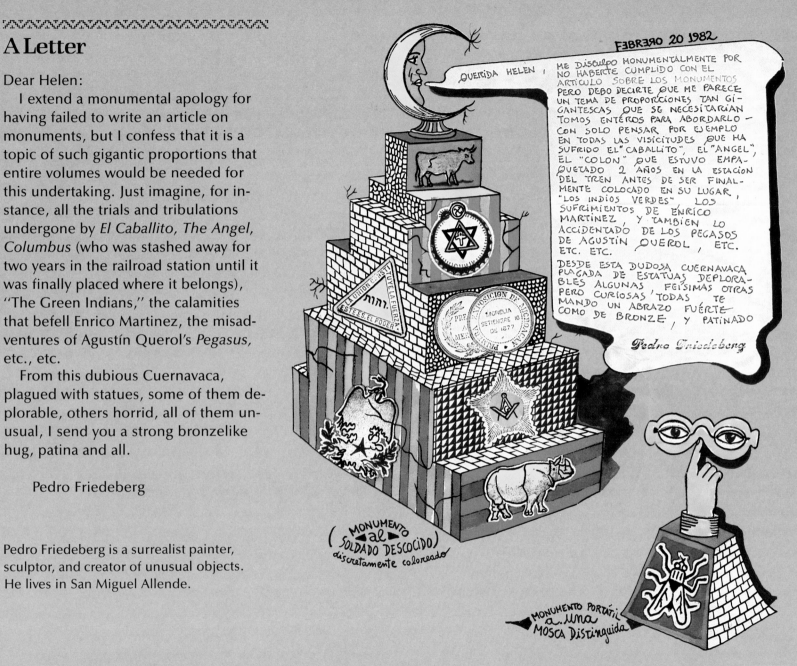

Monument to the Unsewn Soldier
Portable Monument to a Distinguished Fly

Benito Juárez: From north to south, from east to west, in cities, towns, villages, and hamlets, he is there, an inevitable icon.

Juárez Identikit 36

37 *Juárez Identikit*

A Juarez Identikit:

Unrecognizable yet unmistakably all Benito Juárez (a good clue is the bow tie). Usually referred to as Father of the Country, this solid and dependable, squat figure has become the most ubiquitous of national monuments. His best known phrase, *"El respeto al derecho ajeno es la paz"* (To respect others' rights is to be at peace), is a much-used inscription.

The archetypal Benito Juárez, atop the *Hemicycle to Juárez* (1910) in Alameda Park, Mexico City.

41 *Juárez Identikit*   The first of a long line of provincial mutants, in Montemorelos, Nuevo León.

Tlalpujahua, Michoacán

43 *Juárez Identikit*   Polychrome renderings offend the taste of the up-and-coming middle class and are being repainted a uniform coat of silver, gold, or bronze. Still, some multicolored figures can be found in out-of-the-way corners such as Cuetzalán, Puebla.

De Chirico revisited, in Soto la Marina, Tamaulipas.

45 *Juárez Identikit*

The main square of Mineral del Monte, Hidalgo, is an ever-changing kaleidoscope of colors. On subsequent visits we found it completely repainted in equally enchanting hues.

Hidalgo Identikit 46

47 *Hidalgo Identikit*   A lovely art deco corner in Xico, Veracruz; this style, reminiscent of pre-Hispanic geometric stylization, is still alive in Mexico.

Miguel Hidalgo, the archetypal "Father of Independence," in Ciudad Victoria, Tamaulipas.

Hidalgo: An Identikit:

A close second in number of monuments and popularity is Miguel Hidalgo y Costilla. The Father of Independence is always dressed in cassock and black boots and holds either a broken chain or the banner of the Virgin of Guadalupe, under whose aegis he fought Spain and declared Mexico's independence. Easy to make out, with a gentle face, flowing hair, and a balding top, he is the closest competitor in popularity to Catholic saints.

Poza Rica, Veracruz

51 *Hidalgo Identikit*   Acaponeta, Nayarit

On the way to Zacatecas.

53 *Hidalgo Identikit*   San Juan del Rio, Querétaro

A small town in the Bajio, central Mexico.

55 *Hidalgo Identikit*

A corner in Taxco, Guerrero.

Zacatlán, Puebla

57 *Hidalgo Identikit*

El Carrizal, near Coyuca, Guerrero.

As one enters Pachuca, Hidalgo, time gets compressed. Fiberglass copies of pre-Hispanic "giants of Tula" lead up to a futuristic pedestrian crossing; the next couple of miles are littered with at least a dozen monuments in as many different styles. Towns (as well as traffic) have grown tremendously in the last twenty years, and many a place can boast equally triumphal entryways.

THE ICONS OF POWER AND POPULAR ART

Rita Eder

In Mexico, the interminable succession of monuments emerges amid the rediscovery of the vernacular, neoclassic, and modernistic forms, as either allegory or realism.

Monuments can be found in the more conventional sites such as city or village squares as well as in the most unexpected places: a coconut plantation, an inaccessible valley, in the middle of a desert, or alongside a superhighway. At first glance, there seems to be a preponderance of traditional hierarchical figures of the heroes who were enshrined by Mexican history in different eras. Gradually, however, new visages of persons more recently in power have been added to this already substantial list. Despite the jumbled array of monuments, there nevertheless appears to be a plan that ensures the continuity of the

Rita Eder, art historian and art critic, specializes in Latin American art.

republic, an ideology that nurtures the modern nation—at least from the official viewpoint. This is evident in the interpretation of the styles implemented in these monuments. The harshness of these "iron men" who form part of the official government doctrine does not always prevail; sentimental touches based on romantic stereotypes are also used in order to depict them as a combination of philosopher and man of action. There are profound, thoughtful, almost dreamy gazes galore. In other instances, however, the principles of Social Realism are clearly manifested in the informal attire and in certain dramatic gestures hinting at a close kinship between public figures and hard work, at their capacity to abandon the contemplative life and make history.

This phenomenon is so complex and so rich in prototypes that a thorough appraisal of these monuments will produce an analysis of the power structure by clearly defining the political classes. This detailed study of the personalities depicted in these monuments can easily surpass the concept of the tyrant, the *caudillo*, the dictator, or the patriarch so superbly depicted by our Latin American writers. From this angle, one may interpret these stone dummies as "ideological apparatus of the state" and even discover the rhetorical ways of manipulating factory workers, farmers, and other fringe groups.

Certain types of monuments lend themselves to a reflection on the various meanings of kitsch. Just take a look at Ciudad Netzahualcóyotl's main square, with its Disneylandesque representation of our national heroes and the Aztec emperors.[1] This effect is produced mainly by the reduced size and scale of the monuments in relation to the space. Another factor is the disproportion between the base of the sculpture, which can be the throne or the horse, and the personages in question. But perhaps the main reason for the phoniness of it all stems from a peculiar concept of the dramatic. Instead of the choreographed poses from the baroque-romantic tradition or neoclassicism's attempts at endowing the sculptures with human dignity, these monuments deviate from the norm in that the faces look more like the man in the street. The combination of historical credibility, traditionalism, and the commonplace seems to add a comic-strip quality to these monuments.

On the other hand, and in absolute contrast, there are the spontaneous, homemade monuments generally found in small villages, where propaganda gives way to a veritable tribute. In these popular representations, far removed from the more academic stereotypes, craftsmen took liberties to modify and transform a phenomenon that in essence is characterized by its solemnity. One such category of this popular sculpture is devoted to various occupations, where the models were probably inspired by labor symbols that have been erected in different parts of the world under the influence of Social Realism.

As is often the case, the portrayal of our national heroes does not adhere to established canons nor can it be labeled as a manifestation of popular art. Therefore, it is necessary to bear in mind the difference between popular art and the emergence of provincial models or guidelines.

Monuments: Propaganda or Urban Sculpture?

Monuments are none other than symbols created by men in different cultures in order to commemorate, praise, perpetuate, glorify, impose, or destroy a set of values and ideologies. The earliest significance of the monument (menhir) was probably the constancy of death. Later on, the idea conceived by the Greeks and revived by the Renaissance was the exaltation of humanism. During the nineteenth century, with the advent of Napoleon, the monument was used for political propaganda, as instituted by the Romans. This concept is now widespread throughout Western civilization, though it does not exclude funereal or memorial purposes. The monument comprises and is embodied in a multitude of forms; it can be an inscription, a coin, a city, a rock, a great pyramid, or other architectural variations on the same theme such as triumphal arches, obelisks, and so on. Sculpture is but one aspect of this vast and complex universe.

These brief descriptions give rise to two viewpoints: one, that monuments are expressed in accordance with the materials, structure, and dictates of the plastic arts; and the other, that these elements are totally different from works of art. Perhaps this difference is due to the fact that in general, the monument's *raison d'être* is almost always extraneous.

But we are dealing with a delicate subject. Somewhere along the way, between the popular approach to this concept and the theoreticians who conscientiously confront this problem, the basic premises for romantic aesthetics have once again been brought to the fore; not so much because of their aesthetic concepts but, rather, because of the elitist viewpoint on works of art that fosters the idea of inspiration, genius, and its detachment from life for no other reason than to produce aesthetic pleasure.

The demystification of art has become one of the principal factors in defining artistic modernity, and today, the boundaries between what is and what is not art are increasingly ambiguous. The positive effects of this process could well be the democratization of this concept, thus doing away with arbitrary value judgments and hierarchies between major and minor arts, between liberal and manual arts, between art and craftsmanship, and perhaps even between fine and popular art. The social significance and repercussions of art seem to be of more interest than the energy expended in a debate over a definition of what is artistic. However, this also brings about negative consequences such as an avoidance of descriptions and evaluations of the concrete phenomenon itself. There is difficulty in defining the particular structure of the objects we are dealing with, how to analyze their intrinsic nature, how to understand the interplay between their components.

How can monuments be excluded from this controversial issue? Do they merely generate an external significance, are they interesting only from the sociological viewpoint? What do they represent, what do they mean, how are they accepted, who views them, and how are they viewed? Wouldn't these signs necessarily have to be perceived within their own interrelation? How to differentiate the monument from public art? Is it possible to disregard the harmonious volumes and the visual impact of a ziggurat? How to dismiss the link between monuments and urban art, and consequently, the importance of such successful achievements as the baroque Piazza Navona?

It is often said that as of the nineteenth century the aesthetic importance of monuments became irrelevant. That may be true if we cling to the idea of a monument as propaganda, if we accept the populist concept of the monument, if we believe that the inhabitants of large urban centers should resign themselves to the visual pollution invented by some modern democracies: the legacy of neoclassicism adopted by the republic as its official style. These monuments suggest not only the emergence of a new moral code but also new political castes, and, consequently, they have been imposed precisely as a necessary consolidation of power. In modern times, urban sculpture endeavors to abolish the old guidelines for building monuments. It is important to have at least a temporary frame of reference in order to determine, from its particular form and its integration into the particular space, what sector of society its target is and whom it serves.

The Mexican Monument

In order to understand the complex evolution of monuments in Mexico, we will provide a brief outline of its historical development that hopefully will explain their remarkable proliferation.

63   Two monuments on a quiet street in Xilitla, Guerrero, commemorate one sad day. Both tomblike and facing each other from opposite sides of the street, they are dedicated to Gregorio and Fortino Román, brothers who while drunk on New Year's Day, 1956, shot each other to death. The bullet holes are still to be seen on one of the walls.

The Díaz Era

The contemporary history of Mexico's innumerable monuments actually begins with the decree enacted by Porfirio Díaz in 1877 stipulating that a series of statues of Mexican heroes be placed all along the Paseo de la Reforma.[2] During that particular era, whenever heroes were mentioned, there was also the idea of revindicating certain aspects of Mexico's pre-Hispanic past. The Spanish Colonial period (1524–1810), that "dark medieval era," was soon rejected and consequently deleted so that Mexican history resumed with the heroic feats of the Independence movement.[3] The most important result of this decree was undoubtedly the statue of Cuauhtémoc, the last Aztec emperor, created by sculptor Miguel Noreña. Cuauhtémoc, therefore, was the first artistic challenge in a series of nationalistic ventures initiated and endorsed by the Porfirio Díaz regime.[4]

By the end of the nineteenth century, Cuauhtémoc appeared as a symbol of change in artistic categories, in the sense that there was now an attempt to define what was aesthetic, no longer according to the prevailing influence of European art but rather in regard to ancient pre-Hispanic cultures. The complex problem of a neo-indigenous style therefore arose, although toward the end of the century it nevertheless staunchly adhered to the prescribed academic practice of idealizing the face and the body. However, the modernization process is evident in the use of abstract design, such as the pre-Hispanic fret that corresponds perfectly to the emergence of Art Nouveau, based precisely on the predominance of this abstract design.

Cuauhtémoc and the statues along Paseo de la Reforma clearly reflect an idea of national unity where the historical processes are distinctly ascribed to the Porfirio Díaz regime, especially after his first reelection in 1884. The so-called "Porfiriato," therefore, was not merely a period of Frenchified customs and positivist "scientists" but it was also an era that attempted to define its national values within the obvious limitations of its project. Due to the newly developed interest in archeology, the fascination with ancient cultures concentrated on statues with Indian themes. These were undoubtedly influenced by neoclassic principles, as can be seen in Alejandro Lacrosi's interpretation of the Aztec kings Izcoatl and Ahuizotl, cast in 1889. The *Indios Verdes* (Green Indians), as they are now called, were originally placed along the Paseo de la Reforma but have since been transferred to the northernmost point of the city.

The Benito Juárez monument, executed in 1894 and erected in Oaxaca by architect Carlos Herrera and sculptor Concha, not only glorifies the heroes of the Reform movement (1856–1862) but the revaluation of the Indians' contributions as well. In 1906, the year of the Juárez centennial, there was a contest to select the best monument to Juárez and the other heroes of the Reform. The winner was Guillermo Heredia's neo-Doric Juárez Hemicycle. However, Juan José Tablada enthusiastically describes one of the projects submitted by the pseudonymous "Zapoteca." It was considered totally unsuitable by Don Nicolás Mariscal, one of the judges, since it now was no longer just a tribute to Juárez but rather "a monument to the Zapotec civilization." According to Tablada:

This is a patriotic work of art, emancipated from foreign influence as was the work of the Indian liberator. It is a Zapotec monument inspired by the vestiges of this art, which has been revealed to us in the marvels of Monte Albán, and if it has not been sufficiently extolled, it is only because, regrettably, it has been passed over. If Juárez had been a purebred Indian, what would be more natural than to honor him with the art created by the genius of his race? The monument is stark, impressive, invariably Mexican, invariably ours. If indeed "nationalism" has taken root, this is the time when the Indian hero should be honored....[5]

It must be pointed out that this neo-indigenism would be reintroduced in the 1920s, albeit with other characteristics. Meanwhile—between 1889 and 1899—the thirty-four statues along Reforma were being erected. They include members of the intelligentsia, generals from the Reform and Independence periods, the men who drafted the Constitution of 1857, and distinguished poets and physicians. These personages are associated with instilling the official brand of nationalism that has been called the country's religion ever since the time of Justo Sierra.[6] A secular "saints' almanac" was even instituted, with the purpose of replacing the religious calendar, and consequently, historical contradictions disappeared. Monuments, like the murals later on, entrusted the nation's heroes

65

The Monument to Cuauhtémoc in Mexico City. This was the first major monument of independent Mexico, fittingly dedicated to the last Aztec prince to fight the Spaniards. It is one of the few monuments that still stands in its original place on the Paseo de la Reforma. (photo by Hugo Brehme, 1920)

with a mission: that of stressing the successful and harmonious continuity of the system.

The 1920s: The Establishment of Official Guidelines and Their Consequences

If it is true that there is a connecting link between the tradition of modern monuments and the Díaz era (1880–1910), it is also true that it must be distinguished from the period that began after the Revolution of 1910, particularly with the cultural nationalism promoted by José Vasconcelos as of 1921.[7] Generally speaking, the cultural characteristic of this decade was the encounter with its national roots, which made it necessary to resort to pre-Hispanic and popular art. This source, then, became the primary concern of the artists of the period who became well acquainted with the center of anthropological research devoted to the rediscovery of pre-Hispanic pieces on display in the National Museum. The study of these pieces exerted a great influence on official art and on its endeavor to promote a proletarian culture. There was, at that time, a genuine effort to encourage popular creativity. Sculpture was manifested, for example, in reliefs such as those by Juan Hernandez, an unskilled worker who, without any previous training, became an expert woodcarver.

Nevertheless, despite manifestations of a new style of popular sculpture, artists such as J.M. Fernández Urbina and Ignacio Asúnsulo believed that a revolutionary kind of sculpture had not yet been developed, and at that time (1926) they claimed that what predominated was, in fact, the concept of vulgar official sculpture, adding that it was "impossible to introduce a trend that could compare to the forerunners of native Mexican sculpture."[8] Guillermo Ruiz, who agreed with his colleagues regarding the deplorable state of official sculpture, intimated that since it was "the workers who translate our lies into sculptures, they themselves should accept the responsibility." Furthermore, he proposed, "We should work directly on the material itself: wood, stone, bronze, and metals that can be embossed; create new and diverse forms within our own nature, so that the full impact of the work and all it implies will make itself felt."[9]

Direct carving, which as we have seen, was an attempt to create a popular art form, attacked the deception involved in modeling and longed to return to the tradition of "good sculpture," since this was the technique used for ancient sculptures. The followers of this movement attacked Rodin, of course, and pronounced themselves in favor of architectonic sculpture. Simplicity and precision of expression, as opposed to "picturesqueness," were proclaimed on behalf of the skilled carvers who responded to the block. "We must aspire to retrieve a higher, more 'macho' type of art."

The School, which emphasized direct carving, was established with these goals in mind. It was headed by Guillermo Ruiz while Gabriel Fernández Ledesma also taught there. The School had several workshops: ironwork, woodcarving, direct stonecarving, smelting, and gold- and silversmithing. A quick glance at the works produced by the students in this school during the 1920s clearly shows that it unquestionably had popular appeal and that a large number of the non-official monuments now scattered throughout the country originated in these teachings.

Since it was primarily a school for workers and apprentices, it disapproved of art for art's sake, proposing instead "the edifying dynamism of the popular artist," who learned to beat out and twist the iron for making windows, smelt bronze for the venerable heads, or carve wood for a series of doors with historical themes. There was an attempt to emulate the anonymous artisans of the Middle Ages. In some aspects it was a kind of Mexican Bauhaus. During the 1930s, the artists who favored a different kind of sculpture, as opposed to the "official school," were able to produce the kind of monuments they would like to have created in the 1920s: solid, architectonic structures that remained true to the original materials, such as Ignacio Asúnsulo's monument to General Alvaro Obregón (1934), the monument to the Revolution (1933), a joint venture by architect Carlos Obregón Santacilia and sculptor Oliverio Martinez, and Guillermo Ruiz's gigantic statue of Morelos erected on the island of Janitzio in the state of Michoacan (1936). These monuments were characterized by a predominance of forms inspired by the Roman arch and the impressive imitations of entrances to the sacred cities of the Egyptians, while the reliefs reflected a more modest attempt to exalt the people or the martyrs of the republic.

The 1930s can well be regarded as the period when Mexican monumentalism was consolidated in art,

not only because of the hundreds of kilometers of walls painted on by the members of the mural painting movement, but also because of the type of monuments that were built. A new form of creating art had been jelled, and it was manifested with corresponding audacity and maturity: for example, the murals of Orozco, Rivera, Siqueiros, and Tamayo in the Palace of Fine Arts, the Orozcos in Guadalajara's Hospicio Cabañas, while Rivera was immersed in the first phase of his gigantic pictorial epic in the National Palace.

Thus, the production of monuments between the Vasconcelos and the Cárdenas periods was characterized by a quest for a distinctive style in an attempt to understand and apply the formal principles of pre-Hispanic art. However, in the 1930s, especially during the Calles period, it centered around forms associated with the authoritarian regimes of the past, such as Imperial Rome and Pharaonic Egypt.[10] The comparison between this style and certain features of the European art that developed between the two World wars (1919–1939) seems inevitable, due to the emphasis on national cultural values where realism or realisms served both revolutionary and fascist causes.

There is yet another aspect of European art analogous to the Mexican monument. Despite the quest for a breakthrough, for a new and original art form (the innovatio), the concepts of traditional aesthetics were nevertheless preserved. A bird's-eye view of several European monuments will enable us to observe certain similarities to their Mexican counterparts. Take, for example, the monumental nationalism conceived by Mussolini, the Czech sculpture of the 1920s, and,

This statue of Cuauhtémoc crowns the façade of the town hall of Cuetzalán, Puebla.

69 It would seem that the inspiration for this monument at Villa Cuauhtémoc, Veracruz, came from the logotype of the Cuauhtémoc Beer Company.

above all, the resemblance to Soviet monuments, closely bound to Lenin's propaganda strategy devised between 1917 and 1922.[11]

Until the 1940s, the quest for an art that reflected the national essence, particularly in monuments, was, for the most part, an undisputed notion. However, during the Cárdenas and Avila Camacho administrations, several new sculptors appeared on the scene, among them Juan Olaguíbel, who is best known for the Diana and the Fuente de Petróleos (Oil Expropriation) fountains. The variations introduced by Olaguíbel, and particularly by Rodrigo Arenas Betancourt, included emphasizing the human figure more than the pedestal or its base. Furthermore, the human figure itself had lost its rigidity and tended to express private rather than patriotic emotions.

Monuments and Modernity

As we mentioned at the beginning, this approach to monumental sculpture has endured up to the present day. The panorama was nevertheless considerably enhanced; it can even be said that it was unleashed beyond all control. It was not until the late 1950s when its nationalist character finally evolved and artists became more concerned with international movements that monumentalism, as it was understood up to then, began to waver and eclecticism finally came out into the open. Although equestrian statues of some governor or another, Morelos, Zapata, Cárdenas, did not entirely disappear, this period marked, however, an emergence of what we could call "modernized" monuments. Without venturing to define the difficult concept of modernism in Mexican plastic arts, we could well say that its nationalistic isolationism in the arts underwent a remarkable transformation during Miguel Alemán's administration (1946–1952) and was finally consolidated throughout the 1950s. There seemed to be an overwhelming urge to keep up with the urban avant-garde movements. And, while this trend indeed produced excellent results as far as painting was concerned, monument building, on the other hand, adopted the most archaic aspects of internationalism that never quite jelled. Monuments were in a sense like the portrait of Dorian Gray, where the state was eager to project an image of national prosperity and social justice, although the end result would, in fact, enrich the then incipient bourgeoisie and the so-called political class.

The final, and more recent stage in the process of building monuments, is when they are no longer commemorated and become mere landmarks to guide the inhabitants of this unruly metropolis. They represent the conscience of urban growth, an attempt at retrieving the social and aesthetic function, and a serious analysis of their *raison d'être*.

As we mentioned in the beginning, a treatise on monuments raises more questions than can be answered up to now. However, some of these issues may possibly have been clarified through this brief historical review. In the first place, we can appreciate the relationship between the development of monuments and the ideological changes that took place within the Mexican political system. To this effect, it is necessary to depict exactly the opposite image:

70

71   *The Hemicycle to Juárez* in Alameda Park, Mexico City, was erected in 1910 to commemorate the centennial of Independence—with Revolution only months away! (photo by Hugo Brehme, ca. 1920)

Stylistic, simplistic, modernistic, or deco, the idea of the hemicycle persists. The 40,000 ton original has gracefully shrunk to lovely proportions in Ciudad Mendoza, Veracruz (above).

73

The Monument to the Revolution was designed in 1910 in the classic French Renaissance style and was to have been the main hall of the projected new Palace of Congress in Mexico City. Work was interrupted by the Revolution and not resumed until 1933, when the framework was turned into what is today the focal point and setting for massive conventions of the ruling party. Its vast scale has mellowed in relation to the surrounding high buildings.

75   An offspring, in a northern town where Pancho Villa is revered, acts as a base to this unusual portrait of
him sporting a colonial hat that would seem to echo the massive dome of the original.

the idea of the harmonious whole. On the other hand, although monuments contain a demagogical appeal to the idea of nationality and nationalism, nobody ever thinks of actually interpreting these official monuments as the long-term plans of the nation that created them.

The subject of popular monuments is even more intriguing. Although it can be said that the school of direct carving was responsible for consolidating a popular tradition, a great many aspects of this field have yet to be explained. Popular art *per se* entails sponsorships, commissions, orders, bids, and the like, but how to account for the choice of models, the predilection for certain subjects, the liberty that has been taken in regard to materials and color? It is at this point where a vital and up to now overlooked chapter in the history of Mexican art could be inserted: a study of the independent artistic manifestations that ultimately can reveal much more about the complexities of artistic production in Mexico than the entire body of official art.

Translator's Footnotes

1. Located northeast of Mexico City in the state of Mexico, Ciudad Nezahualcóyotl sprang up as a squatters colony. It is now a sprawling, self-contained municipality with well over 3 million inhabitants.

2. A number of monuments were built even before the Díaz regime, of course. Around 1868, shortly after the victory over the French Intervention, Benito Juárez's administration erected statues in honor of Vincente Guerrero, Miguel Hidalgo, and such other famous personages as renowned journalist José Joaquín Fernández de Lizardi (1776–1827). The latter is best known for such political satires as the picaresque novel *El Periquillo Sarniento*. Ida Rodriguez Prampolini, *La Crítica de Arte en México* (Art Criticism in Mexico), vol. 2 (Mexico: UNAM, 1963). 322. (Author's citation)

3. This attitude is reflected in the glaring absence of monuments to the Spanish *conquistadores*, with one exception: the statue of Hernán Cortés commissioned by Don Manuel Suárez, proprietor of the Casino de la Selva Hotel in Cuernavaca. The statue was placed at the entrance to the hotel's then spacious gardens. (Author)

4. Fausto Ramirez, *"Vertientes Nacionalistas en el Modernismo."* (Nationalistic Aspects in Modernism.) Paper presented at 9th Annual I.I.E. symposium, *Nacionalismo y el Arte Mexicano, 1900–1940*. National University of Mexico, January 1985. (Author)

5. José Juan Tablada. *"La ciudad frente al Monumento a Juárez."* El Mundo (February 6, 1906). (Author)

6. Born in the state of Campeche, Justo Sierra (1848–1912) was an outstanding lawyer, educator, historian, writer, and political figure. He occupied a number of political posts, such as minister of public instruction and fine arts from 1905 to 1911.

7. José Vasconcelos (1881–1959) was secretary of education from 1921 to 1924, during Alvaro Obregón's administration, and his clear-cut cultural policy included the establishment of public libraries, popular education programs, book fairs, publications, and extraordinary support of the Mexican muralist movement.

8. FORMA, no. 2 (Mexico, 1924). 7. (Author)

9. Op.cit., p. 8. (Author)

10. Plutarco Elías Calles (1877–1945), who was president of Mexico from 1924 to 1928 during one of the most turbulent periods in post-revolutionary Mexico, was the self-proclaimed "maximum leader of the Revolution." The period known as the "Maximato" also lasted during the administrations of presidents Emilio Portes Gil (1928–1930), Pascual Ortiz Rubio (1930–1932), and Abelardo Rodriguez (1932–1934) since Calles was the veritable

power behind the throne.

11. For Lenin, lining the streets with statues of revolutionary and popular heroes was of vital importance. In his memoirs, Lunarcharsky, who was the public education commissioner at that time, states: "Lenin...intends to decorate the squares of Moscow with statues and monuments in honor of the great champions of socialism." This proposal became a decree, despite artists like Tatlin who knew full well that there was no sculptural tradition in Russia capable of sustaining this program. Lenin's plan to demolish the statues of the czars and replace them with images of socialist heroes did not meet with success. In fact, it was only during the Stalinist era that Russian monumental sculpture came into its own. Two important examples are Vera Mishlina's monument to Work and to the Collective Farmer designed in 1937 and the huge statue of Stalin over the Dnerospestrovsk hydroelectric tower. (Author)

The Monument of Independence, on the Paseo de la Reforma in Mexico City, is the largest of a series of monuments commissioned for the Centennial of Independence in 1910. Its elegance and scale have withstood the onslaught of modern times and the encroachment of skyscrapers. (photo by Hugo Brehme, ca. 1920)

Celaya, Guanajuato

Not surprisingly, the *Monument of Independence* has produced respectable progeny. Occasionally, clusters of the original iconography persist in ever-waning scale and quality, as in the Guadalajara version (right); or just the sheer column may survive, gracefully supporting a Father Hidalgo (left), in Tuxpán, Veracruz.

A close-up of the *Angel of Independence*, not undeservedly
the symbol of Mexico City.

80

81   A scrap-metal rendition of the Angel (shown close up at left) embellishes an exclusive residential area
in Monterrey, Nuevo León.

As any photographer knows, a tripod makes a handy support. This concrete example in Misantla, Veracruz, bears a concrete Motherhood. The *"Hidalguito"* (opposite) in San Jerónimo, an old village engulfed by Mexico City, represents a classical idiom in naïve proportions. But somehow it is delightfully right in the tiny square where it stands.

On Pedestals:

Indispensable decor of a town's main square, local or provincial monuments are often mass-produced effigies of national heroes. Bases and pedestals, however, reflect the ingenuity, or ingenuousness, of the local builder, designer, or craftsman. They frequently mirror their surroundings in the choice of materials, be they stone, tile, or mosaic chip, and their architectural references are often selected from buildings nearby. Sometimes, naïve and inexpensive solutions have more charm than the massive and pretentious impositions of recent years, no matter how professionally designed.

85 *Pedestals*   Though in a similar compositional vein, this haphazard construction in the city of Chihuahua (above) compares unfavorably with the pedestal in Cozumel, Quintana Roo (opposite), lovingly dedicated to a local doctor.

Near Santiago Tianguistengo, State of Mexico, Benito Juárez appears to be sinking in a maelstrom.

87 *Pedestals*   In Las Delicias, Chihuahua, the base for a Benito Juárez monument took the shape of a scroll on which to engrave his famous words. A side view, showing the support elements, gives rise to the local humorous nickname *"el Dolarizado."*

Near Teotenango, State of Mexico, a man-made hump at the foot of Ajusco Volcano is used to display the riding skills of Don Gustavo Baz, ex-governor of the state of Mexico.

89 *Pedestals*   Lava rock loosely cemented supports the head and hand of the great poet Amado Nervo, in Tepic, Nayarit, his hometown.

91   Lighting a monument can be a problem. The spotlights that do not get stolen can transform the image
for better or worse, like hero of the Independence José Maria Morelos (above) getting ready for a
sleigh ride in Chilpancingo, Guerrero.

Brace yourself: the main highway leading south from Mexico City abruptly offers the driver three forks in the road. Under no circumstances must the middle one be taken: it tilts to a vertical and stops dead, right behind a group of giants surveying and drilling the pavement. It is the *Monument to the Roadmakers*.

ES MEJOR MORIR HACIENDO EL BIEN Y NO VIVIR HACIENDO EL MAL
LÁZARO CÁRDENAS

93   Conscientious and complex, the symbolism is all there to commemorate Lázaro Cárdenas and the expropriation of oil, in a hamlet of Michoacán, his native state.

In Veracruz, a base that was, and still is.   94

95   It suddenly appeared on the side of the road, and we did not dare go back for a better look.

Cabezotismo: cabeza, head; *cabezota,* big head:

Cabezotismo: cabeza, head; *cabezota,* big head:
The giant head syndrome is, no doubt, the fault of
the pre-Columbian Olmecs and their huge stone
heads found on the coast of Tabasco. Massive portrait heads of national heroes dot the Mexican landscape; modeled, chiseled, cast in concrete or
bronze, they can be seen for miles. Local humorists
have baptized them with nicknames such as *el tem-
azcal* (the steambath) or *el enterrado* (the buried
one). A landmark of Monterrey, this monument is
normally referred to as "the Turkish bath."

97 *Big Heads*   Mexicans can easily identify the subjects of these portraits even from the rear.

This former president, Benito Juárez, can be found in Mexicali, Baja California.

99 *Big Heads*   Juárez, Hidalgo, and Carranza, in Ensenada, Baja California: they died violently, but not by decapitation.

Father Hidalgo in a square-to-be on the outskirts of the city of Veracruz.

101 *Big Heads*   *President Adolfo López Mateos, Electrifier of Mexico* overlooks the Infiernillo Dam in Michoacán. The man standing at the base is an indication of the scale of the head.

Another portrait head easily recognized from behind by Mexicans: President López Mateos, in Toluca, State of Mexico.

103 *Big Heads*   *The loneliness of power*. This giant concrete octopus, spanning twenty feet, adorns the entrance to an intended residential development in Veracruz.

Benito Juárez in the shape of a triumphal arch. Designed by David Alfaro Siqueiros in 1972, the monument was posthumously completed by his brother-in-law Luis Arenal. Forty feet high (with six tons of sheet iron used in the head alone), it stands off the Calzada Zaragoza, Mexico City.

ON CIVIC MONUMENTS AND THEIR SPECTATORS

Carlos Monsivais

> "An equestrian statue is
> no good unless the orator receives
> a good swift kick from the horse"
> Ramon Gómez de la Serna.
> *Flor de Greguerías*

I Forfeit My Statue

Entourage, fanfare, and photographers. In every town square, our bronzed founding fathers preside over either the end or the beginning of the main thoroughfares, lying in ambush along the highways, remembered only as landmarks. Juárez's head, dispersed throughout, continues to lecture the few misguided Austrian archdukes that may still be around. The figure of Hidalgo carries the Virgin of Guadalupe banner, and originates popular culture. General Mo-

---

Carlos Monsivais is a journalist and writer whose special interest is Mexican popular culture.

relos is situated at the gates of heaven; Venustiano Carranza, the hero of Cuatro Ciénagas,[1] embraces the Constitution of the Republic while Emiliano Zapata reminds us not only of agrarian utopias but of his Hollywoodesque transfigurations as well. Our most prominent heroes take turns sharing the spotlight with homegrown paragons, only occasionally arousing the curiosity of some tourist rather vaguely satisfied by the locals: the general who resisted the invader, the humble craftsman who issued a timely warning and lost his life in the process, the mother who relinquished her sons to the War of Reform,[2] the scholar who burned the midnight oil figuring out the exact date the city was founded. Busts, statues, hemicycles, galloping *caudillos,* statesmen caught unawares while engrossed in deep meditation, founders of various and sundry institutions and martyrs of political stability. "The Nation is highly indebted to...." And so, the decor of the squares and streets is complemented by the Symbols of the Commonplace: in Tampico, the Great Crab divulging its inhabitants' main source of livelihood; in Villahermosa, the statue of a music-hall singer; in Tijuana, the title page of the Free Textbook featuring its buxom, seductive Motherland. The Mexican government's concept of aesthetics consists of blending everything together in a timely symbiosis: martyrs completely subjugated by progress and figures from Greek and Roman mythology corroborating either ambition or misinformation on the part of the governor who presides over the unveilings; lessons in public spirit and unfathomable abstract themes; hallucinations contrived by sculptors determined not to be trapped into any commitments of a chauvinistic nature and stone monstrosities endowed with the beauty of the indispensable. The universe of patriotic statuary.

I Forfeit My Bust

In time (and not a great deal is required, at that), statues, busts, and "allegoric creations" are destined to receive equal treatment as a backdrop for commemorative ceremonies and romantic trysts, proving that excessive recall is but a facet of oblivion, a disproportion that detracts harmony from something that would not have had it anyway.

Monuments represent a number of things: revenge against the vanquished enemy, a sumptuous evocation of the past, political defiance, intimidation, the assessment of historical accomplishments, the exaltation of power that is, in fact, a surreptitious proclamation of the patron's particular taste, a testimony of unpremeditated strength, an admission of cultural naiveté.

There is no country without a statue and no statue without its corresponding sermon. However, and in no time at all, familiarity transforms these sculptures—whose message is extremely clear—into a dubious art form; a folk festival, so to speak. Without actually saying so, it reinforces a compulsory aesthetic concept: we must make the most of what we see, since it will be a long time before it disappears. Indeed, these eyesores destroy the harmony of the landscape and extinguish all hope of visual redemption. But since now it is impossible to get rid of them, the most sensible approach is to discover whether, in effect, they gave rise to an aesthetic concept contrary to that intended by their creators. Statues denounce historical gaps, emphasize the stability inherited from those who died a tragic death so that others could govern without too much trepidation and confirm the threat of commemorative gatherings. Within the generous or restricted number of meters placed at their disposal, statues express the governments' viewpoints (entreaties against losers' amnesia), guarantees of filial affection for those who contributed to the well-being and continuity of the Republic.

Clarity and confusion. It is extremely difficult to arrive at a theory of popular aesthetics in regard to the monuments that have been inflicted on us. In civic sculpture, what is classical becomes picturesque. Moreover, once the hero in question turns up as a statue, he is already self-contained, offering no explanations. He is now officially our contemporary, because he survived extermination at the hands of *caudillos* and dissidents alike; he still rules supreme, much to the astonishment of the masses who don't necessarily know who he was. He is a symbol of power and its interpretations, explicitly stressing the need for the legitimacy of successive governments. (Everyone knows that from their isolated spot in the middle of the municipal square, Morelos, Juárez, and Zapata prove that all historical periods are, in fact, only one, and that in peacetime the only conceivable epic is respect for authority.) Statues, however, fail to provide us with a different kind of information: who looks at them and how; how much do they actually tell us about the collective sense of history and of aesthetic perception in spite of it all; what part do they play in urban and didactic life; what was a hero at the turn of the century and what is a hero now; how does the appreciation of monuments increase or diminish in everyday circumstances; how can beauty be materialized and how does "official art" become invisible?

Clarity and confusion. Who actually likes statues aside from their significance and who is capable of deriving aesthetic enjoyment only from something completely unrelated to civic duty? In order to approach patriotic statues and recognize their merits other than those acknowledged by the government, we must first recall how these heroic sculptures are integrated into their context, the manner in which urbanization destroys the slightest trace of pedagogy and incorporates governmental objectives into the one-and-only aesthetics of desolation.

There Is No Nobler Art, No Truth So Live

In nineteenth-century Mexico there was a popular axiom: "In spite of being staunch republicans we must admit that there is no nobler art than sculpture." The "nobility" of sculpture does not stem from aesthetic criteria but, rather, from its conspicuous presence, from its role as society's first intruder in a public space—a domain that up to then had been occupied only by the Church. The exceptions—statues of monarchs and viceroys—only attest to the link between power and divinity, extending the attributes of religious sculpture to the lords of the land, primarily its spectators' reverent credulity. If it was difficult for painting to emancipate itself from ecclesiastical influence by endowing its secular themes with the pious overtones of a parable, sculpture, on the other hand, achieved its "secular autonomy" almost immediately—a political feat claiming its share of the public's veneration, which in Mexico, as in every other country, synthesizes the process that transforms historical content into governmental actions.

So, within this framework, each bust, each monument, fulfills a commemorative function: history is a succession of events and persons who proceeded with courageous intensity as long as they were canceled out as alternatives. Every statue is a tribute to what has endured, to what will never occur again. A statue represents the struggles it has undertaken and those it has ruled out, the regime that vindicates it as well as the regime that opposes it. This is why, from the destruction of Baal to this day, practically the earliest recorded event marking a people's liberation is the destruction of monuments honoring heroes and leaders who have suddenly ceased to be so. The eradication of statues is a phenomenon that usually precedes new constitutions. Right from the start, may those loathsome, appalling atrocities topple over, may these sinister effigies come crashing down, may iconoclasm be enforced by dint of the pickax or dynamite only to be immediately dissolved.

Blind faith in allegories is boundless. Ever since the earliest years of Mexico's independence from Spain, there has been a demand for representations of a triumphant nature. In 1822, the National Pantheon was instituted, while the 16th of September and the 28th of August (Agustín de Iturbide's saint's day) were proclaimed national holidays. Iturbide, our "first Emperor," by the way, started the custom of self-congratulatory celebrations. Consequently, the dictator Porfirio Díaz (who ruled for over thirty years) added September 15, his birthday, to the secular calendar. A blatantly offensive mockery still remains in the Plaza Mayor, the hub of both temporal and eternal concerns, where the great artist Tolsa designed and executed the equestrian statue and the elliptical balustrade immortalizing the nonexistent feats of King Charles IV.[3] In a Mexico where sovereignty was so recent, symbols were anything but symbolic. On the eve of his ascent to the throne, Agustín de Iturbide ordered that the statue of Charles IV *(El Caballito)* be covered with a blue globe to prevent him from witnessing the ceremony.[4] Thus, deprived of all pomp and the outbursts of power, it was hidden from view until 1824, when the first president of the Republic, Guadalupe Victoria, regarded its proximity to the National Palace altogether too offensive. Shortly before the statue was to be turned into a balustrade, politician Lucas Alamán rescued the bronzed affront by alleging its status as a work of art, and managed to have it transferred to the Colegio de Mineria where it remained, in virtual imprisonment, for a considerable period of time.[5] Antonio José de Irrisarri, a Spaniard, observes:

By so doing, the Mexicans wished to exhibit

108

109   King Charles IV of Spain, packed and ready to move again.

their patriotism, and so they did, with their characteristic lack of common sense....What sign of servility was this? It was a reminder that the Kings of Spain had ruled Mexico, but if all memories should be erased, in that case, it would have been better to throw all the gold and silver coins into the ocean, since they proved that the Fernandos, the Carloses and the Felipes who governed Spain during the past three centuries were kings in Mexico, and after flinging these coins into the ocean or into the depths of hell,.every single book alluding to the Spanish conquest in that country should also have been burned; the Viceroy's palace, the Cathedral, the University, the Colegio de Mineria and all the other buildings erected by kings should have been demolished....

Irrisarri is persuasive but not altogether convincing. The endemic awe of statues is not necessarily the reason for their rejection. While awaiting the circumstances that will consolidate them, these symbols enjoyed considerable prestige in a developing society and in a city devoted to monarchical and ecclesiastical obedience—or in more turbulent times to endless grumbling. Once the animistic habit of visualizing Spanish monarchs in anything bronze was finally overcome, the new nation's visual apprenticeship and the theories nurtured by tradition were reinforced. The theory contending that "It is not man who creates symbolism, but rather symbolism that constitutes man" is both corroborated and disproved here. In nineteenth-century Mexico, the crowds gathered around allegorical representations of a nation that, at first glance, consists mainly of poems, patriotic anthems, marches, proclamations, edicts, sculptures, and fiestas where representation is the very essence of history and society. Leaving Charles IV in the Plaza Mayor instigates a retrospective form of obedience, or, better still, it demonstrates that either through laxity or incompetence a new nation is incapable of devising symbols of its own. There is one widespread, predominant idea: let's create a country out of the blue, sustain it with deep-rooted, renowned traditions, and little by little let the symbols themselves be both incentives and goals; a statue is a historical symbol transformed into a political platform.

The great Liberal writer and politician Ignacio Manuel Altamirano, in his prologue to Guillermo Prieto's *El Romancero Nacional* (1888),[6] takes this factor into consideration when he complains: "We have a very small number of national monuments, whether due to internal wars, or whether the best materials have priority or because the press and the artists themselves were not zealous enough in promoting the construction of public monuments to our heroes, and lastly, perhaps due to apathy, which is the very essence of our nature." Altamirano lists the catalog for 1885:

The statue of Hidalgo in Toluca (private donation)
The statue of Morelos commissioned by the Emperor Maximilian, which Juárez later had transferred to the San Juan de Dios square
The statue of Vicente Guerrero in San Fernando

Square

The statue of Hidalgo in the city of San Luis Potosi

The humble cenotaphs commemorating Hidalgo in Chihuahua and Morelos in Ecatepec

The (imminent) statue of the last Aztec Emperor Cuauhtémotzin on the Paseo de la Reforma.

And that is all. There are no statues in the provinces; the example set by the government of the state of Morelos where the official seals "reproduced the image of the exalted leader whose name it bears" has not been perpetuated, and no one paid the slightest attention to the appeal for a mausoleum "where the ashes of our national heroes could be laid to rest." Altamirano then concludes:

Thus, in a nation where there are no monuments to immortalize the memory of its heroes and where there is scant information about them, it is no wonder that national epic poetry has not flourished. On the contrary, it is truly amazing that among the more cultured classes there is any trace of history or tradition still left. In regard to the more ignorant sectors of the population, try this little experiment: ask anybody, whether an illiterate Indian or a mestizo who speaks Spanish and can read, about the Virgin of Guadalupe or the patron saint of such and such a town and he will immediately tell you the story or the legend of the saint's miracles. Then ask him about Morelos, the Galeanas, Mina, Guer-

rero, the Bravos, the Rayón family, Valerio Trujano or Pedro Ascencio, and he will merely shrug his shoulders, not knowing what to reply. There is barely a faint recollection of these people in the very places they made famous with their heroic feats! This discrepancy is due to the fact that the Church has always made sure that the object of cult is kept alive in the people's imagination day after day, kindling their religious sentiment through their teachings on these traditions.

When this is not accomplished by resorting to objectivity and storytelling, the people are unjustifiably deprived of their history, of their traditions, of their religion itself.

Altamirano was straightforward while explaining what was to serve as the guideline for the government: to imitate that model of wisdom, the Church. The national heroes had to be literally sanctified, invested with the aura of infallibility, to ensure their place in the Hereafter, so that the popular imagination would never get rid of them and so that these secular saints could endow the Nation with the miracle of their existence. It is far from easy to compete with the omnipresence of Catholicism, which even capitalized on something called "classical taste," so eloquently displayed in nineteenth-century sculpture riddled with proselytizing criteria, where saints and pagan gods alike are intermingled and where, as ordained by ecclesiastical tolerance, there is a profusion of plaster-of-Paris reproductions of classical themes and works: Ganymedes and Venus de Milos and Winged Victories

The slain Juárez in marble, on his tomb in the Panteón de San Fernando, Mexico City.

and busts of emperors. Nymphs fall into the aesthetic category and virgins into the didactic.

The religious theme is all-encompassing since it is derived from exemplification. Pelegrin Clavé, the highly esteemed art teacher and painter, advised his disciples: "Endow each one of your works with the appropriate attributes as long as they are always Christian, since you have had the good fortune to practice your art under the celestial auspices of the august religion that exalts mankind, destining it to eternal contemplation of that infinite truth that is, at the same time, infinite beauty." The devotional aspects are therefore complemented by the classical, paving the way for the heroic. Cupids and saints. Mercury and *Imago Pietatis*, Christs crucified and gladiators. Classical culture forms the bridge between religious and secular society, and such allegiance to the Hellenic and Roman ideals creates a dream world where writers Bernardo Couto and José Joaquin Pesado are commemorated in togaed busts similar to those of Ancient Rome, and on the verge of saving the Empire. The Greco-Roman gods, hand in hand with figures from Christianity, serve to define the criteria: civic statues must be in the classical in style. In 1873, Manuel Islas concluded the series of marble statues *La Patria* (The Motherland) and *Juárez*, where Don Benito in a shroud could easily pass for Julius Caesar. Friends, Mexicans, countrymen, lend me your ears. I have come to praise Juárez, not to bury him.

Sculpture is a living political and moral phenomenon. A statue in the Alameda gave rise to angry protests and exacted a reply from the editors of *El Partido Liberal* January 17, 1890, reproduced in Ida Rodriguez Prampolini's *La Crítica de Arte en México en el Siglo XIX.*):[7]

Those so-called Catholics, just like the people we are dealing with now, must harbor an excessive amount of malice *inpetto*, in order to emit such a scandalized protest, believing that the innocence and chastity of our children is imperiled by looking at a statue of Venus in the Alameda.

Why have these pious souls kept silent about the wax Infant Jesuses displayed nude in their crèches and kept in some homes for what they call their nativity scenes? Undoubtedly because they are dolls, most of them somewhat deformed, who cannot inspire the same sinful thoughts as the life-sized statue of a woman, especially if it has artistic merit. Do these pious souls ignore the fact that the veil sometimes used by prudes to cover even the Infant Jesus or some of the larger statues only serves as greater temptation, or is it enough to cover nudity with a veil such as theirs to morally cover their hypocrisy?

The Independence Monument

"It is as though he had led the flourishing circle of illiteracy along the path of mysticism."
Gerardo Diegi, *Fabula de Equis y Zeda*

Stone, marble, and political stability. First and foremost, Porfirio Díaz retrieved the idea of exemplarity from the liberals' penchant for extracting the unalterable lessons of the past. Throughout his dictatorship

Two versions of Don Venustiano Carranza, at left in Toluca and above in Veracruz.

A thirty-foot-high Cárdenas on the Avenue Lázaro Cárdenas in Mexico City.

he was to unleash the invasion of statues, at that time irrefutable evidence of the advent of the nation's maturity. Every great monument was assigned the task of reconciliation, of doing away with factions, of support to the regime. For example: sculptor Miguel Noreña's statue of Cuauhtémoc on Paseo de la Reforma and Insurgentes was unveiled in 1887. At long last, there was an Indian hero to represent—not ethnic pride (unthinkable in Díaz's time) but, rather, the beginning of a reconciliation with the past. "He was an Indian, but he was an emperor."

The vast site selected for this didactic display was the Paseo de la Reforma. Every state in the nation was expected to deliver two statues of generals, of martyrs averse to collective amnesia, and of prominent educators. And to top it off, of course, was the statue of Cuauhtémoc, the beginning of an "ornamental nationalism" that (though not exactly lavish when it came to pre-Hispanic figures) would nevertheless generate the aesthetic metamorphosis of a "not very prestigious" civilization. There were other Indians back then—the message implied—handsome, arrogant, and strong, totally different from the sorry breeds who now merely vegetate. This selective procedure engendered not only the monument to Porfirio Díaz by Adamo Boari (creator of the Palace of Fine Arts project), which never materialized, but also the dreamlike imagery of painter Saturnino Herrán.

To General Díaz, unveiling statues and laying cornerstones were the fundamental trappings of political stability. He gave his blessing to everything that seemed destined to endure. In his plan for Mexico's Centennial celebrations, statues and busts and memorial monuments played a vital role. The orgy of unveiling ceremonies involved a ritual: the Dictator standing next to the Figure being commemorated, then a poem recited by a prominent figure, with the corresponding flock of hangers-on, then applause, and finally the city was distinguished by yet another hagiographic reference. Just take a look at the agenda for September, 1910. On the 9th, the inauguration of the monument to Queen Isabella of Spain. On the 11th, the cornerstone for the monument to General Washington was laid and the statue of Louis Pasteur (courtesy of the French colony) was presented to the general public. On the 13th, strictly controlled rejoicing at the new effigy of Baron Humboldt (a gift from the emperor of Prussia, Wilhelm II). On the 16th, the *pièce de résistance*, the long-awaited event: the unveiling of the monument to the Independence, the work of architect Antonio Rivas Mercado, which according to some is a jewel of neoclassicism, while for Antonio M. Bonet it is a masterpiece of formal traditionalism that is purely Mexican. During the ceremony, poet Salvador Díaz Mirón read an ode to "The Good Curate."

Hidalgo, it is not because I am clever,
that I am so inspired
to compose a paean
to your noble feat
and in speaking thus, I struggle
to do so skillfully,
thus I lift my voice in praise

119   President Díaz Ordaz of ill fame (1968), who could only be put up safely in his native state, seen here in
Ciudad Serdán, Puebla.

The statue of President Miguel Alemán adorning the campus of the National University was dynamited twice and then boarded up for repairs. This protective casing was transformed into a collective revolutionary mural in 1968, and the whole thing was then finally removed.

which by no means
is worthy of such a grand occasion.

The diplomatic corps turned out to pose for the official photograph in full regalia—hats and outfits imported from Paris especially for the occasion. It was made perfectly clear: the obscure country conceived by Hidalgo now glittered under Porfirio Díaz. On the 18th of September the Juárez Hemicycle was unveiled amid these manifestations of historical gratitude. Foreign Relations Minister Luis León de la Barra reported on the cost of the monument: 390,685 pesos and 96 cents. On the 20th, it was the gift from the Italian colony that was exposed to view: the monument to Guiseppe Garibaldi.

According to the spirit of the times (a euphemism referring to the tastes and the standards set by the ruling class), statues were regarded as a means of communication, which explains the hieratic ostentation of politicians when they are portrayed, since not only do they bequeath their image to posterity, but, as living statues, they also impart precise instructions to the sculptor. Porfirio Díaz is far from being the exception to the rule. He knew that all of America was overrun with statues, and was well informed, to the last detail, on the sovereign powers' faith in their monumental souvenirs. Every mausoleum, every republican sphinx, every tomb vouches for the cities' aesthetic aggrandizement, for the Nation's gratitude, for the permanence of the person responsible for the tribute, for merging a past crammed with heroic exploits and a present whose

121   National heroes often display a sneaking resemblance to the president then in charge. José López Portillo, a riding enthusiast, is disguised as Father Hidalgo in Salazar, State of Mexico (left), and as Morelos in Ciudad Serdán, Puebla (right).

greatest feat is not to allow any heroic exploits at all. Monuments, therefore, should be memorable, massive, conspicuous. That is why they aspire to the condition of prototypes, literally overwhelming versions of the power and the glory. The Independence monument and the Juárez Hemicycle not only commemorate themselves, but they also sum up a cultural policy and a political culture, a prelude to the Mussolinian pomp and platform that, in some form or another, would be pursued by the regimes of the Mexican Revolution. Statues are a guarantee of social peace; as long as we keep unveiling them, it will be a sign that the roster on the memorial tomb to the heroes on the battlefield has been filled, and that nobody wears military boots any longer, except when posing for an artist.

And You, Josefa Ortíz de Domínguez,[8] Go Quietly Back to Your Dais

The cult to the statue, whether in Moscow or in Wichita, is an international language, a rapid and emphatic metamorphosis of historical processes. The contribution of countries like Mexico is the transformation of political expedience into an inadvertent form of aesthetics expressing the public taste. "Well, that's a fine-looking statue," says the mayor (governor) (president) to the sculptor. The patron is not lying; he is fascinated by its stately bearing, by its *panache*, by the striking resemblance. (It's as though Morelos himself had posed for you.) Then, this rigid and contrived aesthetic concept soon blends into the landscape in the most unexpected forms, losing its heroic qualities and acquiring a familiarity that eludes the critics. It becomes so well known that it is actually endearing. And so endearing that it becomes invisible.

The nation that emerged in the 1920s availed itself of monuments and statues to reinstate the commemorative ceremonies in honor of its heroes, constituting, as a result, the chain of public ordinances. Once again, these tributes were transformed into a school for misinformation or, in a few rare cases, into examples of sculptural innovations. The public taste was corroborated by kitschy household decor; towns and cities were devastated by these lessons in civics, vital spaces were rendered useless, didactic attributes were conferred on a number of veritable eyesores, and Carlyle's theses were carefully observed. There they are, either astride a horse or else waiting for the entourage to present them with a floral wreath. Hidalgo, Morelos, Juárez, Zaragoza, Carranza, Madero, Villa, Zapata, Obregón, Calles, Cárdenas…Not one of them has been spared from the monumentalism of the nation's (inventoried) gratitude, although probably not many among them would really have wanted to be spared.

In this visual give-and-take, for every burial mound erected another is canceled. With no colossal stone and cement tributes, with no plaques or busts attesting to the citizenry's gratitude, one would have lived in vain. The excluded sectors were resentful, and went overboard on their irritation, as can be seen by the frenzied fetishism exhibited by the reactionary group known as the *sinarquistas*.[9] According to Alfonso Taracena in *La Vida en México bajo Miguel Alemán*,[10]

122

123   López Portillo rides on in Monterrey, this time as himself.

Famous union leader Fidel Velázquez survived eight six-year terms as secretary general of the Federal Labor Union. Of this statue in Monterrey, the sculptor Cuauhtémoc Zamudio says: ''That is how I see him, monolithic, a stone.''

on Sunday, December 19, 1948, 2000 *sinarquistas* congregated around the Juárez Hemicycle and attacked the personage depicted therein. The head of the *sinarquistas* for the Federal District, Rubén Mangas Alfaro, harangued: "The so-called age of Reform and Revolution is the age of shamelessness and ignominy, and that great scoundrel Juárez was responsible for all the vileness there is at the present time, because he devoted himself to robbing churches, like the Corpus Christi Church we are facing now." In this historical overview, there is something for everyone: "Hidalgo, the treacherous, drunken, opportunistic priest"; "Morelos, the sinister agitator in the service of heretical tendencies." Then came the moment of "secular desacralization": a young *sinarquista* climbed up Juárez's statue, spat three times on Don Benito's head, and covered it with a black veil. The master of ceremonies, Carlos Gonzalez Obregón, justified this act: "*Sinarquista* youth had covered Juárez's face because we do not want to set eyes on this rogue, nor do we want him to look at us." Never have civic monuments been so convincing. The *sinarquistas* believed they actually saw Don Benito; consequently, the authorities, acknowledging that the Nation had actually been physically attacked, deprived the *sinarquistas* of their voters' registration permit and ultimately outlawed them. Was this an interplay of symbols with not-so-symbolic results? It was, rather, the conviction that statues are, unquestionably, a form of political instruction and a corroboration of public aesthetics. In the first instance, the Government of the Mexican Revolution admires and controls its predecessors and founders (or whoever it may regard as such) and openly proclaims that statues are what they are and what they represent. If, in passing, art and the aesthetic elaboration of history can also be fostered, well and good, but are the nations' leaders concerned about the continuity that includes them: will the future take me into account or not?

You have to get involved in politics, so that in the future it is clear that these men made History. That is why, in 1951, President Alemán authorized (and probably insisted on) the colossal statue perpetuating his capacity as a lawyer, his status as a civilian, and his role as a creator of the new Mexico. There, surveying the campus in his cap and gown, clutching a wealth of knowledge in his hand, *Licenciado*[11] Miguel Alemán confidently awaits the ovations from future generations. His faith in the strength of the system is such that he does not regard his statue as an affront but rather as a bequest. He does not foresee—because he considers it absurd—the probably premodern era of ingratitude that, as of the late 1950s, would be manifested against this statue in the form of demonstrations, protests, repudiations, and attempts to blow it up, only to become an ephemeral mural in 1968: on the barriers protecting the partially destroyed statue, a group of painters expressed their collective and individual support of the student movement.

"My, But Doesn't the *Licenciado* Look Like His Statue!"

More recently, as far as civic monuments are concerned, the emphasis has been on personal vanity and aesthetic feasibility. If we have a shortage of museums, if artistic education in our schools has either been so deficient or, in fact, nonexistent, if "monstrosityism" provides the key to "popular taste" if the unbridled urban growth does not immediately assimilate any monumental proposal, regardless of its quality, then it is good to acknowledge that civic sculpture and its fierce complement, "civilian sculpture" (gigantic crabs advertising seafood restaurants, fantastic animals for publicity purposes) are endowed with irrefutable evidence. Forerunners of art (and reminiscent of a glimpse at neoclassicism far removed from any attempts at avant-garde), these pieces of frozen heroism or heroic salesmanship are, in some way, essential to this society. The State needs them: they are historical and geographical references; they represent loyalty to the past and loyalty from those present during this solemn ceremony. They are indispensable to society as represented by government officials and businessmen, in keeping with the public taste that has been duly concentrated and accumulated there.

Fortunately—or unfortunately depending on one's urbanistic outlook—public, civic, and "civilian" sculpture still constitutes a strong link between the community and its appreciation of the formative spectacle and the gigantic or "outside-the-home" aesthetics. If in the nineteenth century sculpture was an instrument of secularization (where there was a saint, there is a hero; where there is a hero there will be a saint), in the twentieth century sculpture is the technique of behavior modification (where there

is a hero there is an ideology; where there is an ideology there will be a catalog of permissible attitudes) and of aesthetic appreciation as a subsidized form of indifference. Beauty is everything that belongs to the past: in museums, in newly refurbished squares, or harbored in the inaccessible chambers of the very rich. With very few exceptions, whatever you may see will not be beautiful. It will be, at best, nice.

The sculptors' enthusiasm is irrelevant. Familiarity divests all statues, busts, and sculptural complexes from any artistic content whatsoever. In the end, there is only one standard: the criteria of permanence—whether for a popular idol (the statue of Pedro Infante,[12] erected from a pile of old keys collected for that purpose) or for a live politician. In Monterrey, observe the ten-ton bronze statue, four-and-a-half-meters tall, of Fidel Velazquez, secretary-general of the Federal Labor Union. (The statue is conceived just like this: "Very monolithic," says sculptor Cuauhtémoc Zamudio. "This is exactly what Don Fidel's physique and personality remind me of: a rock." In Tianguistengo, State of Mexico, the statue of Carlos Hank González, former mayor of the Federal District, measures 2.6 meters and weighs eight tons. In the nation's capital, the statue of ex-president Luis Echerverria; in Tijuana and in Campeche, the equestrian statues of ex-president José López Portillo. "Look," says the mayor of Tianguistengo to the reporter, "Professor Hank is extremely pleased....He knows that this is a modest token of appreciation for all he has done for us." (*Proceso*, January 26, 1981). Modest or not, as far as politicians are concerned, the statue assumes the indisputable status of an homage: either to the System or (in the fortuitous case that he may still be among us) to the person. After almost two centuries of not keeping a safe distance between statues and reality, between statues and immortality, the widespread conviction is finally expressed: without sculpture Coatlicue would be just one more shadowy figure from the pre-Columbian period.[13] The vanquished gods also promote themselves through sculpture.

A deluge of statues! A dictatorial succession of founding fathers, paragons, benefactors of the nation and of one's hometown, quintessential geniuses. Anything possessed of (some) merit must be immediately transposed into the real and figurative language of sculpture. Without this, there is no guarantee for high-mindedness; the noble feats that demand our gratitude simply do not exist, either on a local or on a national level. Civic and "secular" sculpture have done considerable damage to the development of sculpture in Mexico (an extremely effective medium for "artists" like Octavio Ponzanelli, who created the bust of General Arturo Durazo[14] and the "Greek statues" in his Parthenon). It has, however, shaken the very foundations of urban perspectives in terms of a popular axiom: in Mexico, historical and traditional values are determined by the number of allusive statues (the undisputed winner: Benito Juárez) and by the fact that these monuments and busts succumb to the omnivorous onslaught of urbanization.

Iconoclasts, beware. Heed the advice from Jean Cocteau: "The risk of being a destroyer of statues is to be turned into one."

Translator's Footnotes

1. Venustiano Carranza (1859–1920) was born in Cuatro Ciénagas, Coahuila, where later on he was to hold the office of mayor. His active political life, which included the governorship of his home state, culminated in his presidency in 1917, when the current Mexican Constitution was promulgated. However, a revolt headed by Plutarco Elías Calles, Alvaro Obregón, and Adolfo de la Huerta forced him to flee the capital. He was assassinated by the troops of General Rodolfo Herrero in 1920.

2. The name "War of Reform" is often accorded to the searing conflict between Conservatives and Liberals as a result of the controversial Reform Laws promulgated by Benito Juárez's government in 1859, centered mostly on the separation of Church and State and the confiscation of Church property.

3. King Charles IV of Spain (1748–1819), a weak, ineffectual king, easily influenced by his advisors, was responsible for, among other things, selling Louisiana to France in 1800 and for obtaining considerable revenue from charitable works through a royal decree issued in 1804. When Napoleon's troops invaded Spain in 1808, he abdicated in favor of his son, Fernando VII. He died in exile, in Rome.

4. Obviously, the real purpose of the globe was to prevent the people from seeing the statue of the king.

5. Lucas Alamán (1792–1853), a staunch conservative, served as foreign relations minister from 1830 to 1832 and

again in 1853 during Santa Anna's last presidential period. One of his most noteworthy actions was to grant immunity to runaway slaves from the United States once they crossed into Mexico. A prolific writer, he is best known for two controversial works on Mexican history.

6. Guillermo Prieto, *El Romancero Nacional* (Mexico: 1878). (Author)

7. Ida Rodriguez Prampolini, *La Crítica de Arte en México en el Siglo XIX*. (Mexico: UNAM, 1967). (Author)

8. Josefa Ortíz de Domínguez (1768–1829) was one of Mexico's few acknowledged heroines of the Independence movement. She was born in Valladolid (now Morelia, Michoacan) and married Miguel Domínguez, *corregidor* (mayor) of Querétaro in 1791, hence the affectionate name of "La Corregidora" by which she is now remembered. Both she and her husband were sympathetic to the cause, and his political position enabled her to play a decisive role in overthrowing Spanish rule. When the plot was discovered, however, her husband locked her in the house, but she managed to warn the conspirators. She was sent to one convent and then another as a form of imprisonment, and in 1822, upon her release, she was offered the post of lady-in-waiting to the empress (Iturbide's wife), which she refused.

9. The right-wing *Unión Nacional Sinarquista* was founded in 1937 and registered as a legitimate political party during the Lázaro Cardenas administration, and it received considerable support from the Church. However, as a result of the skirmish at the Juárez Hemicycle, the party's registration was canceled in 1948 during President Miguel Alemán's regime.

10. Salvador Novo, *La Vida en México en el sexenio del Presidente Miguel Alemán* (Mexico: Empresas Editoriales, 1969). (Author)

11. In Mexico, as in a number of Latin countries, professional titles such as *Licenciado* (Lawyer), *Ingeniero* (Engineer), and *Arquitecto* (Architect) are commonly used and are considered a status symbol of sorts.

12. Pedro Infante (1917–1957) was a popular screen and singing star and a true idol. Even now, over thirty years after his death in an airplane crash, mobs of people continue to flock to his grave.

13. An Aztec goddess, mother of Huitzilopohtli, the principal Aztec deity, Coatlicue may have either symbolized the mother giving birth, or may be an amalgam of various feminine deities. Now on display in the National Museum of Anthropology, Coatlicue was buried after the conquest and was unearthed during the late eighteenth century. However, it is only in this century, largely due to reappraisals by anthropologists and art critics such as Justino Fernández, that Coatlicue's significance and artistic merit have been truly appreciated.

14. Arturo Durazo, Mexico City's notorious chief of police during López Portillo's administration (1976–1982), left the country after his tenure ended, but was eventually extradited and is presently awaiting trial on several charges, including illegal possession of arms and "inexplicable wealth," as, for example, the lavish "Parthenon" he had built for himself in Ixtapa, a popular resort on the Pacific.

129   Mayor Hank González sits modestly, pensive as a poet, in the square of his hometown, Santiago Tianguistengo, State of Mexico.

The *Fuente de Las Tarascas*, a monument to the indigenous Indian tribe, stood facing the colonial aqueduct of Morelia. Its realistic polychrome coating so offended the local moralists that it was removed to the agricultural fair grounds, to be replaced by a plain bronze copy.

131   *Mayahuel*, the goddess of the maguey plant, fittingly adorns a square in Tequila, Jalisco, where tequila comes from.

Heroes of Independence (or the Conquest of Space?) in Dolores Hidalgo, Guanajuato.

132

133   The inscription on this monument in Culiacán, Sinaloa, reads: "Come back with your shield at your side, or on top of it. This phrase synthesized the heroic spirit of Spartan mothers, and it was repeated twenty-five centuries later in Sinaloa by Agustina Ramírez, who sacrificed twelve sons to the Homeland."

A menacing Cuauhtémoc, the symbol of Indian resistance to the invader, welcomes tourists who dare to cross the border into Tijuana, Baja California.

Aztec to Zapotec: A Mexican Primer:

Aztec Revivalism is rampant in local statuary, but so is neoromantic, postindigenist, pseudocolonial, neoethnic, Disney kitsch, and Hollywood modern. Purists might yawn, but wondrous inventiveness is certainly evident. To make complex patterns simple, let us begin at the beginning (please flip through the following pages for an instant history of Mexico):

135 *Mexican Primer*

At the entrance to a Social Security hospital in Jalapa, Veracruz, Cuauhtémoc might appear to have turned into a symbol of the medical profession.

Oh, Mexico City, City of Palaces, we the Aztecs have arrived! . . .
In the background, the National Palace.

to sit and ponder . . .
The new city hall of Ciudad Netzahualcóyotl, State of Mexico, is spread around a square in the form of climbable pyramids.

139 *Mexican Primer*

. . . *in awe and askance at our lot in life:*
The Monument to ''The Race'' in Mexico City.

we were leaders . . .
Near Merced Market, the conquerors of Tenochtitlán are being boated around, and the laying out of
Mexico City begins.

141 *Mexican Primer*

and are now bossed around.
The Conquistador, in Monterrey.

We merged and were submerged . . .
Monument to the "Mestizaje," the mingling of the races, in La Villa, Mexico City.

into awareness of sin.
Fray Bartolomé de las Casas, seen here in Monterrey, was a staunch defender of the human rights of
American Indians, but he approved the importation of Negro slaves.

Go north, young man!
The Pioneer, in Monterrey. The colonization of the North of Mexico and most of the southwestern
United States is a feat without parallel on the continent.

145 *Mexican Primer*

. . . a prayer in your heart

La Ermita, near Lagos de Moreno, Jalisco. There is no end to roadside shrines, which sometimes
commemorate a fateful accident.

The Virgin at your side . . .
On the old road to Cuernavaca from Mexico City, a Virgin of Guadalupe, Mexico's patron saint, made of painted stones and shells.

. . . though you may die by hanging.
Jesús Malverde, a bandit hanged in 1909, is the object of unofficial popular veneration in Chihuahua City. A patron saint to contemporary thieves and smugglers, his shrine is littered with stones and pebbles thrown to him for luck.

Blessed be the Pope who lives in Rome . . .
A huge concrete and stucco spire dedicated to Pope Pius IX in the village of Jamay on Lake Chapala.

149

. . . as You bless our poor wealthy dead.
Jardines del Recuerdo, Mexico City. Cemeteries are big business.

A marker near Taxco, Guerrero, commemorates a battle that ended in a handshake.   150

151   *Morelos loves the spring*, on Janitzio Island in the lake of Pátzcuaro.

The Morelos of Montemorelos, Nuevo León (above), keeps an eye on the United States border, 150 miles to the north.

A flagpole at its most minimal, in a hamlet near Taxco. No school is without one.

A more elaborate example is to be found in the schoolyard of San Miguel Tecuilapan, Puebla.

155   The Mexican family is united around a flagpole in Ciudad Mante, Tamaulipas (left). There is no limit to how elaborate a flagpole can get, as in Fresnillo, Zacatecas (right).

To the Soldier, on the Periférico freeway in Mexico City (above) and on the way to Pachuca, Hidalgo (opposite).

Literally hundreds of monuments commemorate the *Niños Héroes*, the seven boys who defended the castle of Chapultepec alone against American invasion in 1847. According to legend, the last one alive wrapped himself in the Mexican flag and jumped off the parapet rather than surrender. This monument, in Toluca, State of Mexico, is naughtily referred to as "The drunken lad" or "The bed of stone" (the title of a famous song by Cuco Sánchez).

159   The Cerro de Guadalupe near Puebla, the site of the only battle the victorious Mexicans celebrate, is littered with monuments; this one is the biggest so far.

Emiliano Zapata gallops in, *frame left*, at Hacienda de Chinameca, Morelos. This marks the very spot where Zapata was treacherously ambushed and shot.

160

161   *Zoom in to extreme close-up*. The iconography of revolutionary heroes is often influenced by western movies, as here in Cuernavaca, Morelos.

Fast cut to Pancho Villa in Chihuahua (above) and in another northern town (facing).

The inscription on a monument in Toluca (page 216) could also apply to this one in Cuernavaca: "Zapata has not yet removed his riding boots!"

Whoa!
Pachuca, Hidalgo.

A legend in his native state of Morelos (many of his descendants and relatives are still around), Zapata is depicted here in Atotonilco showing his gentler side.

166

And icons trundle on. A float made ready for a parade, near the presidential residence in Mexico City.

The peaceful village square of Axixintla, Guerrero, as it must have been . . .

WHO COMMISSIONS MONUMENTS?

Jorge Alberto Manrique

The very existence of a civic monument presupposes the prior existence of the person who commissioned it in the first place. In the privacy of his studio, an artist can of his own free will create a given work, even though admittedly this free will may be conditioned by various extraneous factors. He would not, however, normally carry out projects for civic monuments had he not been commissioned to do so or if he had no prospects of obtaining such a commission. Even if this were not the case, the monument would not actually exist unless there were a specific request for its execution. Thus the commission is conditioned by the possibility of the existence of what we call civic monuments. Consequently, it can be safely concluded that the objectives and requirements of

Jorge Alberto Manrique, an art historian, is a fellow at the Institute of Aesthetic Studies, National University of Mexico.

. . . before the intruder.

whoever commissions a made-to-order monument play a vital role in its construction. The patron imposes certain characteristics on the monument indispensable to the function he expects it to fulfill, at least those he considers necessary: a reasonably good dose of "realism" and the dignity demanded by the effigy of a hero. The patron also determines other characteristics that depend on his budget and his interest in the monument, such as its dimensions and materials to be used.

The forms in which the patron's goals and requirements are manifested in the monument itself open up a world of possibilities, ranging from the establishment of the basic ground rules and the wording for an open contest to the extravagant and even ludicrous sponsorship of a close friend. But who, after all, commissions these monuments? As a matter of fact, the backer who provides (not always exclusively) most of the funds for civic monuments is the public authority itself, at its various levels and in its numerous capacities: federal, state, municipal governments, decentralized agencies, etc. It is not the only sponsor, of course, because there are also religious monuments (the Church may perhaps be considered a kind of public power with its corresponding levels as well: from the bust of the local parish priest to the monumental sculpture of Christ the King). There are also commissions from other sectors: universities, citizens' groups, Lions and Rotary clubs, and so forth, although this proportion is negligible compared to work commissioned by civil authorities. The fact that a public power is the main source of capital for this project constitutes a decisive factor in defining the universe of monuments.

It has often been said that the military and civilian heroes of the secular republican world have been gradually replacing the saints. They, too, have their iconography, their attributes, their exemplary role, their purity, and the corresponding legends and historical facts to certify them. The civilian state needed its own list of saints and martyrs, and there were even people such as our own Carlos María de Bustamante, who, in the early nineteenth century, compiled the new "secular year" just as others had compiled the religious calendar centuries before.[1] A precise, fixed calendar, every bit as rigid as its ecclesiastical counterpart, was then instituted. We cannot possibly imagine Juárez without his dress suit or Don Miguel Hidalgo without his frock coat and boots nor Allende without his cocked hat. Don Benito Juárez's features have reached such a degree of standardization that they are instantly recognizable even when interpreted by a number of different artists in a wide variety of materials, from plastic ashtrays to the massiveness of granite, from the solidity of bronze to polychrome concrete.

On the other hand, as far as the "form" of the monument is concerned, there is no dependence whatsoever on religious imagery. The monument is officially regarded as a separate category from that of the saints in their niches. They hark back to the statues of royalty or prominent leaders that appeared during the Renaissance and mannerist periods, which, needless to say, have their own precedent in the

A monument to childhood, not yet unveiled.   172

statues of Roman emperors and outstanding personages of the time. The latter are, incidentally, related to the religious public monuments of ancient times. Among us, however, it is the religious monument that now imitates the civic monument.

If our monuments derive from the statues of princes, liberalism and the modern republican trends brought about an important change in their connotation. Formerly, it was the prince himself who ordered his image to be cast for reasons of his own (other than mere narcissism, although that, too, may have been present), so that his greatness and power could be admired by the people (albeit a subjugated and placid people), secure in the stability and authority of their monarch. In the late eighteenth century, Viceroy Branciforte's petition to Charles IV to erect in Mexico an equestrian statue of the king alleges the need for proving his greatness and reinforcing the submission of his people during that turbulent period. The result was sculptor Manuel Tolsá's *El Caballito,* one of the first great Mexican civil monuments. While not chronologically the first, it was certainly the first in quality. (It must be pointed out, although it will be mentioned further on, that this sense of subjection and peacefulness based on the power of the chief of state has recurred in the recent past as well as in present-day Mexico.) Although the liberal state takes a dim view of the personalistic glorification of the powers that be, it never loses sight of the monument's *raison d'être.* Whenever the state retrieves a hero from the past and exalts him in a statue, it provokes public admiration—and supposedly the emulation of heroic virtues, just as the images of the saints should produce these very effects on the faithful. However, while transferring this admiration to a dead man, preferably one who has died a violent death for his country, the state itself is thus ratified and validated. It is no longer the prince who orders the monument to be built, but it is the state that orders it for itself, in the effigy of the great men it acknowledges as its founders, creators, or champions.

Hence the controversy that sometimes centers around the project for a new monument; a monument to a hero determines the character of the government in question. A case in point is the persistent absence of the conqueror Hernán Cortés in public monuments and the endless bickering that ensues every time it is proposed. The self-image of a government that dedicates monuments to Cuauhtémoc, the last Aztec emperor and defender of his people against the conqueror, is entirely different from the image projected by a government that erects monuments to the conqueror himself. The monument, therefore, acquires a dual significance to the community. On one hand, the fact that it is a public monument—that is, an unavoidable object within the urban or rural context—transforms it into a visual proposal vis-a-vis the community itself, particularly since it always occupies a privileged spot and a prominent position. Although it is normally accorded a passive reception while it is being incorporated into the network of landmarks that constitute the urban universe, it may, however, be rejected, either eventually or straight away. (Only on rare occasions does this rejection persist, as in

Charles IV of Spain has hopefully come to rest. Sculpted in 1803 by the great Spanish architect Manuel Tolsá, and a symbol of Spanish rule, the statue has been moved a number of times since Independence, and now, decontextualized, it is endearingly known as *"El Caballito,"* the little horse.

the case of the statue of ex-president Miguel Alemán in Mexico City's National University.) On the other hand, a monument always embodies both a proposal and a definition of the governmental power that made it possible. Obviously, since monuments are elements in a given political rhetoric, this does not necessarily mean that the subjects on the pedestals concur with the government that enshrines them, but, rather, that the relationship may be quite the opposite. For example, a government that has deviated from constitutional legitimacy in a given historical moment may very well extol the defenders of constitutionalism.

The heroes in the traditional sense, that is, those who founded or defended or reformed the government, are the persons most frequently honored in these monuments. Quantitatively speaking, the cultural heroes rank considerably lower in importance and cover a wide range, from the baroque poet Sor Juana Inés de la Cruz[2] to the popular composer Agustín Lara. Another characteristically Mexican feature—which, if not actually invented by us, has certainly flourished and come into its own here—is the custom of dedicating monuments to abstract concepts or entities or to particular or generalized virtues. Peace, for example, is a universal theme, but others such as mother, the railway worker, the fisherman, the *huapango* (a popular folk dance), etc., are peculiarly Mexican. In these cases, the government glorifies itself in the guise of a symbolic personage or an abstract entity, in an obvious attempt to identify itself with the people. Thus, like the people themselves, the government extols the virtues of the Mexican mother or the fondness for a particular folk dance. Since the authorities who order these monuments belong to different levels, the selection of the subject to be honored in a monument depends a great deal on this factor, whether it be men, ideas, or symbols.

The country's innumerable squares, boulevards, parks, quadrangles, intersections, promenades, and boardwalks are swamped with statues of several popular national heroes. There is no point in naming them. There are other heroes, however, also fellow citizens, who are not as famous and who are to be found mainly in their birthplaces or in the sites where their historical presence was particularly noteworthy, such as Mariano Escobedo[3] in the state of Nuevo León or General Ignacio Zaragoza in Puebla.[4] The message conveyed here is local pride in the special relationship between the hero and the place itself. At any rate, there are heroes or virtues or symbols peculiar to every region. In this case, the rationale of the local or municipal authority is an attempt to prove to residents and outsiders that even a small town has something or someone worthy of being honored by a monument.

When the decision to erect a monument issues from a national authority, the predominant attitude seems to be that of confirming its pact with the people and legitimizing itself before the nation via the hero or the concept that is extolled. Another important factor is to determine whether this public object is the most suitable way to achieve this goal, or if the monument's rhetoric unduly attempts to replace other, more substantial elements in the renewal of this pact.

175

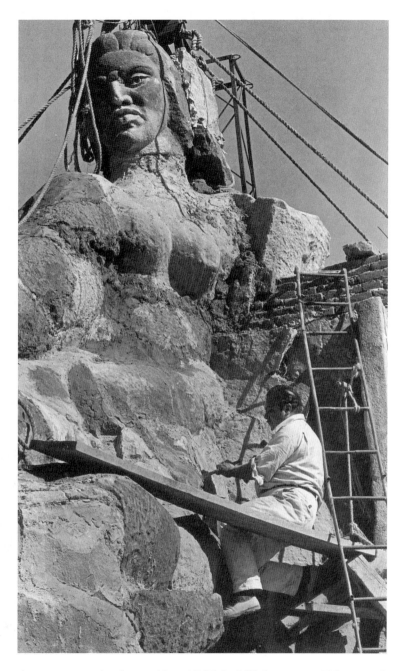

A fairly recent deviation from the norm is for the head of state to either order a monument built to himself or to agree to such a project. This is a clear case of regression to the original purpose of the royal monument, where the monarch in all his splendor comforted, reassured, and inspired his people. There is another type of deviation that becomes more frequent as the monument's patron descends in rank. In this case, the political interests involved no longer adhere to the clear-cut relationship between the ruler and the people he governs but are now warped by the intent to flatter the man in power in order to obtain certain personal benefits for the patron as well as for the community in question. Consequently, there are countless proposals for monuments to the president, to the governor, to his father, or to his relatives if they can even remotely be considered likely subjects for a monument.

Strictly speaking, the monument must fulfill the requirements of the person who orders it. It is, of course, essential that the subject be recognizable. Therefore, a hefty dose of "realism" is indispensable: a bushy beard, a hook nose, spectacles, thick lips—no one is spared. The subject must also possess the characteristic attributes of a hero that, aside from their symbolic representation, also help the public to identify him, like, for example, a military uniform (whether from the Independence era, the Reform period, or the Constitutional army), a sword, spurs, a topcoat, and the book or scroll of the legislator. The pose and gestures must also be in character:

A monument in the making (1966) in Villahermosa, Tabasco, that never made it and no longer exists.

In this foundry in Mexico City, heads, torsos, sectioned or completed, lie in rows ready to go. Usually modeled as mini-maquettes by the sculptor, they are enlarged by skilled craftsmen.

impassioned and expressive if it is a battle-scarred general, or dignified and solemn in other cases, so as to inspire respect. The dimensions and the materials to be used are determined by financial conditions, although not in the abstract sense but, rather, in direct relation to the estimated political benefits obtained from the investment. In view of these characteristics, everything else is perfectly valid, as far as the patron of the work is concerned. Generally speaking, there are no preconceived notions about the other formal components of the work, although perhaps there may be a vague idea that it is "preferable" for it to be "modern."

Once the project is under way, the artist's main problem is how to combine extreme realism (spectacles and all the attributes and gestures of the subject) with the artist's own prerequisite that the work be up-to-date. This dilemma explains the motley collection of monuments in Mexico.

We must also stress that the pecking order occupied by the persons who commission these monuments, and consequently the difference in financial resources, determines not only the size and the materials but the choice of artist as well. This does not mean that the artist's remuneration has any significant bearing on the total price of the monument, but, rather, a small-town mayor's budgetary limitations place him at a disadvantage when election time rolls around. Nevertheless, it would be quite wrong to surmise that the huge monuments commissioned by the higher-ups are better than those ordered by the more unpretentious provincials. More often than not, the statue of a local hero, built with cheap materials and a great deal of candor, reveals not only a greater degree of integrity but a far better compatibility with the surroundings. One will never cease to wonder why such costly, great (in size, that is) monuments commissioned by powerful figures often fall into the hands of mediocre artists. It will be less surprising if we bear in mind that open competitions for this type of project are few and far between. In general, it is the authorities themselves who make this decision, without any kind of contest or technical advice from the appropriate committees. Incidentally, the few contests that have been held did not produce very gratifying results, such as the one for the Independence monument in the town of Dolores, but who knows whether that may be due to the contest regulations themselves, incompetent judges, or apathy on the contestants' part. As a rule, however, any competition of this type should certainly be expected to yield a better quality of work. Besides the absence of qualified judges and committees, there is another factor detrimental to the question of monuments. If they must possess the dubious qualities of realism we mentioned previously, a number of talented artists reluctant to make these concessions are bound to be driven away.

David Alfaro Siqueiros in his studio in Cuernavaca working on parts of the Polyforum in 1967. 180

Translator's Footnotes

1. Carlos María Bustamante (1774–1848) was a prominent and brilliant writer, lawyer, publisher, and statesman from Oaxaca who played a vital military and intellectual role in the Independence movement and was one of Iturbide's fiercest critics when he declared himself emperor.

2. Sor Juana Inés de la Cruz (1651–1695) is recognized as one of the outstanding figures in Mexican literature. Sor Juana was a veritable child prodigy who astounded the viceroy's court with her brilliance. As a woman of the Colonial period, she opted for the religious life as a path to intellectual expression, a choice that often came into conflict with her love of knowledge. Her literary works include poetry, plays, and essays.

3. Mariano Escobedo (1826–1902), a native of the state of Nuevo León, began his military career as a soldier during the North American invasion of 1846. He led a number of important battles during the French Intervention, and organized an army that played a vital role in northern Mexico. Benito Juárez appointed him general-in-chief of operations. He was twice governor of San Luis Potosí and of his home state, and then was appointed minister of war. When Porfirio Díaz rose to power, Escobedo left the country. He tried to lead a revolt against Díaz, was imprisoned, and later on was appointed to Congress, the post he held when he died in 1902.

4. Ignacio Zaragoza (1829–1862) was one of the great military leaders in support of Juárez's policies during the War of the Reform. Zaragoza's victories were mainly in the northern cities of Saltillo, Coahuila, and Monterrey, Nuevo León. In 1861, he was appointed minister of war, but left this post shortly after to command the Ejercito de Oriente (Eastern Army) against the French, a campaign that culminated in the famous Battle of Puebla on May 5, 1862. He died of typhoid shortly after this triumph.

The Spanish Conquistadores took as many local women as they liked, and how prolific! Mothers are often portrayed with heavy Indian features.

Motherhood 182

183 *Motherhood*

In the north, Mothers become distinctly Caucasian, even to their painted fingernails, as in this example in Ciudad Delicias, Chihuahua.

185 *Motherhood*

Motherhood:

Many Mexican mothers are single, a lot of the men polygamous, and that is why Motherhood is the pillar of family structure. Monuments to the Mother are endless. We collected inscriptions:

To the one who loved us before knowing us.

Mother, you are love, holy love,
a love almost immortal, a love without name,
in which man's insatiable heart,
finds infinity in same.

Papantla, Veracruz

187 *Motherhood*

Coatepec, Veracruz

The newly inaugurated Main Plaza in Monterrey can boast at least a dozen monuments.

189   *Oh, what a beautiful morning, oh, what a beautiful day!* Saddleback Mountain, barely visible through the smog of Monterrey, is the backdrop for *Water, Fount of Life*.

Tied to his post, a scrap-iron worker in the industrial section of Naucalpan, Mexico City.

Work:

Childhood is soon gone, and in its place is the pride and hardship of survival. Miners (they die young), soldiers, laborers, railroad workers, oil drillers: the tough professions are well represented by monuments. Road-builders on the new roads, fishermen in seaside towns, firemen, policemen— the one we never found represented, the "*campesino*," or peasant, is the worst off.

Pulling his load. A miner in Pachuca, Hidalgo.

Work 192

193 *Work*   On the highway to Toluca from Mexico City stands a monument to *The Roadbuilder* (opposite and above).
The sculptor is a Spaniard befriended by former president López Portillo in Caparroso, Spain, the
birthplace of his grandfathers. He is responsible for a number of very large monuments all over the country.

A gold panner modeled by the well-known sculptor Ignacio Asúnsolo in Parral, Coahuila. We were directed to it by a local policeman who described it as "a man in his birthday suit, covering his spare parts with a soup bowl."

Work 194

In Guanajuato, a mining town.

197 *Work*   *To the miner*, in Mineral del Monte, Hidalgo (opposite), and in Angangueo, Michoacán (above).

To the Fisherman, in Mazatlán, Sinaloa (above), and in Ensenada, Baja California (opposite). *Work* 198

199 *Work*

To the Customs Officer (above and opposite, left), in front of the Customs House in Tampico, Tamaulipas.

Work 200

201 *Work*

To the Fireman, in front of the local fireman's building,
San Luis Potosí.

A monument to soccer players in front of the local stadium, Guadalajara, Jalisco.

Play:

Well, life is not just toil. Think of anything you like doing, seeing, petting, gobbling up; think of sports, music, dance, fiesta, football, fishing, sailing, singing, bullfights, cockfights, you name it; there is hardly a thing Mexicans have not built a monument to.

A monument to jai-alai, in front of the local casino, Tijuana, Baja California.

Over the main gate to Mexico City's bullfight arena, a group by Humberto Peraza, who is famous for his bullfighting bronzes.

205 *Play*

A monument to the song *"La Mazatleca,"* in Mazatlán, Sinaloa.

Agustín Lara, Mexico's most popular composer, in Veracruz.

A monument to Pedro Infante, renowned movie actor with a great voice, in Guamúchil, Sinaloa, where he was born.

The plaque on the sculpture reads:

AGUSTIN LARA
EL MUSICO—POETA,
QUE TUVO EN LA MUJER
TODA UNA FUENTE
DE INSPIRACION
Y CUYA OBRA MUSICAL
L   A DE ROMANTICISMO
T SSENDIO EN EL MUNDO
VIVE EN EL RECUERDO
AYUNTAMIENTO DE MONTERREY 74—76
XEAW ORGANIZACION ESTRELLAS DE ORO,S.A.
JULIO DE 1975

209 *Play*   Agustín Lara, famous for his love songs, in Monterrey. A can of beer is often placed (empty) on the iron piano, and occasionally his songs are played through nearby loudspeakers.

The Singing Cricket of *Cri Cri*, nom de plume of a famous radio figure of the forties, in Chapultepec Park, Mexico City. Loved by everyone who was once a child, his songs are evergreen.

In a residential section of Cuernavaca, this representation of a macaw—which is known for its stridency—
is perhaps an apt choice for the area.

Delicious cold with fresh lime juice, superb in bronze, in Campeche. The conch (opposite), in Cozumel, Quintana Roo, we recommend *"en escabeche con chile habenero."*

212

To be or not to be, a bust of Benito Juárez in Atlacomulco, State of Mexico.

MONUMENTS, BILLBOARDS, AND GRAFFITI

Nestor García Canclini

The majority of the visual messages found in a city have been imposed. Urban order and most of the architecture, particularly the greatest in size and presence, are the result of governmental or private decisions in which the average inhabitant plays no part. Advertisements (that never-ending programmed renewal of our heart's desires) attempt to force anyone who rides through the streets to think and react according to the consumer-oriented code of economic power. The residents have no say in regard to the nature, content, variety, number, or diversity of these messages. It is up to other people to set the guidelines and determine the degree of realism, pop art, or kitsch and the aesthetic and conceptual order that will prevail.

Nestor García Canclini is a sociologist at the National University of Mexico who specializes in fine and popular art.

Captions courageous, Zapata in Cuernavaca, Morelos.

Who Cares About Monuments?

Monuments are almost always the result of an imposition on the part of political authority. The simultaneous control over public finances, urban space, and official interpretation of history turns the state into the exclusive (or almost exclusive) trustee of the consecratory enterprise involved in erecting these monuments and of the capacity to carry out the project. Since direct intervention from the people is restricted to major political appointments and since government officials and legislators usually take action without consulting the people who elected them, it stands to reason that the choice of site, subject, and basic features of these monuments will be passively accepted by the city dwellers, without its ever occurring to them to exert their critical sense. A monument tends to appear overnight and is taken for granted; drivers and pedestrians go around it, regarding it with even greater indifference than billboards, which generally are more stimulating. However, the research for this book has discovered dozens of monuments that conflict with these statements. Although an imposed historical sculpture and the imposition of commercial advertisements do indeed exist, we can also detect the complex interplay between both systems as well as the interaction between these systems and other forms of expression, graffiti, and the many variations generated by the people themselves. The practice of interpreting the underlying message behind each monument should also be extended to other manifestations of urban life: what actually takes place during this intermingling and the mutual influences of one aspect over another. These contrasts and contradictions tell us a great deal about a city's constant historical transformations.

Notes for a Typology

Although the research conducted was certainly far from exhaustive, we did discover eight principal types of modifications displayed by monuments in relation to the urban context:

1. Neutralization or alteration of the monument's significance due to a disruption in scale: for example, the bust of Juárez in Atlacomulco, which once harmonized with the surrounding buildings, was ultimately devoured by the water tower placed right next to it—fifteen times taller than the monument!

2. Neutralization of the monument due to commercial saturation of the context: the bust of Hidalgo in Tamazunchale, Hidalgo, is engulfed by ads for an establishment that "repairs radios, record players, and stereos," a circus poster, Coca-Cola billboards, and a motley cluster of foodstands, etc.

3. Obstruction of the iconographic message due to the proliferation of urban street signals. For example, on an intersection in the town of San Miguel Allende, the statue of Ignacio Allende competes with five different signs: "La Ermita" (in the shape of an arrow), the name of the street, another arrow indicating the traffic flow, a right-of-way sign, and finally another arrow pointing toward the city of Celaya. The second photograph corresponds to a huge statue of Zapata at the entrance to Toluca. Its base is plastered with four traffic signs, their arrows going every which

Zapata in Toluca, State of Mexico (above left); Zapata in Cuernavaca, Morelos (below left); Ignacio
Allende in San Miguel Allende, Guanajuato (right).

way, surrounded, in turn, by six placards with a variety of slogans. Ex-president Luis Echeverría's quote, inscribed at the base of this monument, is therefore completely hidden from view, while the symbolism of the monument itself is considerably diminished.

4. Subordination of the historical monument to the connotations of an adjoining commercial advertisement. Here, two elements, originally belonging to two entirely different sign systems, are now linked by their proximity to each other and by their reference to the city where they stand side by side. The "colossus of Tula" and the clock bearing the Ford automobile logo, both welcoming us as we enter the city of Pachuca, remind us of the two principal aspects of this city: the pre-Columbian and the industrial. However, the sheer size of the second symbol clearly overshadows the first; the clock, representing the value of time in industry, absorbs the historical significance of tradition depicted by the colossus. Another example is the monument to Zapata directly facing an ad for Taxco's most characteristic hotel: Zapata, the political-popular symbol par excellence, subordinated to Borda, the name that stands for two eras of power in the same region—mining and tourism.[1]

5. Semantic conflict between a historic element and an advertising slogan. The statue of Carmen Serdán next to the curvaceous Phillips model.[2] The television set versus the rifle; the inscription "heroine of the Mexican Revolution" and the sign "I'm your girl in living color"; from the belligerence of the combatant to the sexual availability of the starlet;

Toltec tic-toc. A fiberglass copy of a "giant of Tula," at the outskirts of Pachuca, Hidalgo.

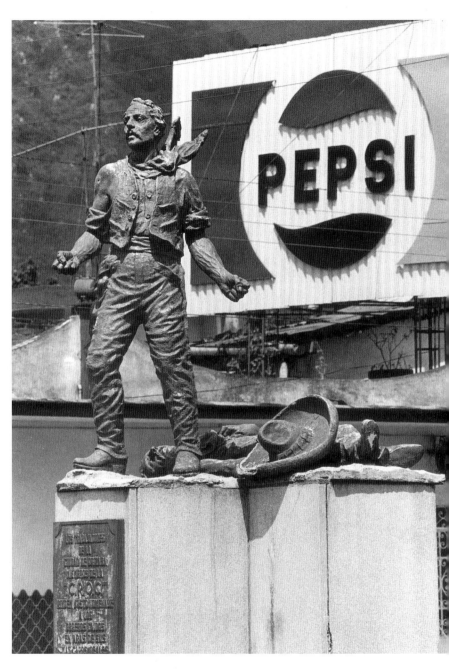

Carmen Serdán in Orizaba, Veracruz (above left); "Salon de Belleza" (beauty parlor) juxtaposed with a well-combed-out Hidalgo (usually identified by the bald spot) in Misantla, Veracruz (below left); and fallen workers in Rio Blanco, Veracruz (right), commemorating the uprising that sparked the Mexican revolution.

from politics to erotica. In short, the history of the revolution and television commercials are presented as two opposite (or complementary?) areas in symbolic elaboration.

6. Ironic implications of a historical symbol by association with advertising jargon: Hidalgo's flowing tresses on the monument next to a "Beauty Parlor" sign; the eloquent statue of the "fallen worker for the sake of his most cherished revolutionary ideals" alongside the huge Pepsi billboard. An even sharper contrast: the monument to Juárez, whose name inscribed below is linked to the word "Gigante," the name of the supermarket that serves as a backdrop to the statue, minimizing it in the process.

7. Ironic implications of a historical symbol through its relationship with the urban context: the statue of Guillermo Prieto, his hand outstretched in one of Mexico City's busiest intersections, earned the popular sobriquet "the man hailing a taxi."[3]

8. Popular intervention as political commentary on the significance of the monument: a host of slogans criticizing the government, the "electoral farce," corruption, etc., are scrawled along the statues to the heroes of the Independence and the Revolution. Another type of strong modifications to the interpretation of monuments derives from the presence of the people themselves: demonstrations against current issues often take place either opposite the sculptures recalling some glorious event of the past or representations of timeless symbols, such as a group of feminists bearing placards in favor of abortion congregating in front of the monument to the Mother.

"Taxi!" Paseo de la Reforma, Mexico City.

A mini version of the gigantic *Cristo del Cubilete* near Guanajuato.

The conceptual juxtaposition among three distinct approaches to maternity is also manifested in the contrasting styles: the anguished woman in the poster alluding to abortion and death; the triumphant smiles of the feminists in their struggle; and the statue of the woman with her son, her grim pride accentuated by her hieratic stone features.

All the cases described refer to monuments that have been dwarfed or subordinated by the urban sprawl. Is this their inevitable destiny? In the research done for this book, there are at least two types of monuments that show the conditions under which they can withstand both social and population changes and even originate a whole new set of meanings:

a. Sculptural pieces that are not, strictly speaking, monuments, in the sense that they do not commemorate anything in particular, which in time become a recognizable landmark in a given site. In Mexico City, the towers at Ciudad Satélite are one of the best examples of this phenomenon.[4] In these instances, we could well say (while their force is still felt and despite the constructional and commercial expansion of their environment) that these sculptures are monuments to themselves as long as every time we pass them they recall the same aesthetic experience we felt the very first time we ever saw them.

b. Monuments not modified or diminished by urban expansion either take on new meanings or become local points of reference. It may be a fountain or an artistic sculpture that became a monument through its capacity to identify and fit into a social space, as, for example, the fountain that gave its name to a

223

The "giant" Juárez in front of the Gigante department store on Division del Norte, Mexico City (above).
A demonstration in favor of abortion adjacent to the *Monument to the Mother*, Mexico City (below).

Rush hour. President López Mateos directs traffic on Zaragoza Expressway, Mexico City.

restaurant at the entrance to Córdoba, Veracruz.

However, both monuments cited are atypical. What to do with the monuments *per se,* those commemorating the independence of a country, the heroes of yore, the patterns and conventions of national thought? Is it possible to disengage oneself from habit and tradition while paying them homage? Is it possible to win the fight (unequal in every respect) against the new system of signs? These questions, of course, call for a more thorough and extensive analysis of this subject.

Symbolic Struggles for Power

The development of capitalism has distributed objects and signs throughout specific sites: currently used merchandise in stores, relics from the past in museums, and objects of purported aesthetic value in art galleries. The messages conveyed by merchandise, historical and artistic works, along with the pertinent instructions for their application, are assigned to educational institutions and the mass media. A meticulous classification of objects and the language used to refer to them maintains the systematic organization of social spaces where they are to be consumed. This precise order structures the consumers' life, indicating their behavior patterns and forms of perception according to each particular situation. The inhabitant of a modern city is able to distinguish among what is purchased in order to be used, what is remembered, and what is symbolically enjoyed; this is a person subjected to the compartmentalization of social life by the corresponding power groups.

However, this impeccable order is constantly disrupted by the street. In the public life of a city, mercantile interests are interwoven with historical, aesthetic, and communicational aspects. The semantic struggles to achieve neutralization, to obstruct other messages or alter their meaning, to subordinate everyone else to their own logic, are dramatizations of the conflicts among the various social forces: marketing, history, the State, and advertising as well as the people's struggle for survival. Whereas the objects in museums are extracts from history (frozen in the sense that they are self-contained in an eternity where nothing would ever occur again), monuments, on the other hand, are open to urban dynamics, enabling history to interact with the new developments in social life and to revitalize its great men thanks to the irreverence of propaganda or of city traffic. They then continue in their struggle against the social movements that outlived them. In museums, the heroes of the Independence are meaningful because of their association with the heroes of the Reform and the Revolution; on the street, however, their significance is constantly renewed through the interaction with present-day contradictions. Without showcases or guards to protect them, the monotonous, lifeless stones of urban monuments are linked to the prevailing anxieties of the modern age through graffiti or mass demonstrations.

Nevertheless, it is obvious that the symbolic life of the city no longer centers around its monuments. Collective experience is represented and condensed by a new system of symbols that correspond to pres-

First come, first served, Taco Bell just ahead, Pancho Villa in Chihuahua.

226

ent-day social relations. City dwellers identify themselves more readily with the specific symbols that embody certain technological values (superhighways, streamlined buildings) and with gratifying consumerism (large shopping centers, supermarkets, recreation centers). Incidentally, it is precisely in the midst of this flurry of modernization that steel, marble, and stone monuments—due to the sturdiness of their materials and the vitality of their forms—attest to the permanence of national identity and historical events, to the continuity and the recollection of their origins. In fact, the difficulties confronted by those monuments that convey strictly historical messages in order to identify places now governed by functional logic, are not merely limited to the monuments themselves. They constitute crucial issues in cultural policy: how to integrate traditions and values of the past with the predominantly pragmatic social practices of the present, whose significance is by no means stable.

What Makes a Monument Popular?

Graffiti, billboards, monuments: three manifestations of the main forces that affect a city. Monuments are almost always the instruments used by political powers to enshrine the principal heroes and the pivotal events of the State. Billboards attempt to synchronize daily life with the interests of economic power, while graffiti—as well as political posters and mass demonstrations by the opposition—express popular criticism of the imposed order. That is why advertisements and superimposed graffiti that either conceal or contradict these monuments are so meaningful. On one hand, the proliferation of advertisements smothers historical identity by attempting to dispel the memory of its people in the anxious, random perceptions offered by consumerism at every turn. On the other hand, in addition to their explicit message, the authors of these spontaneous legends are saying that monuments are ill-equipped to express the people and that the lure of consumerism is hardly enough to enhance their lives. What is better proof of the distance that exists between a government and its people than the need to rewrite their monuments' political message? Is there any statement more eloquent as to the confrontation between commonplace and official events, between what is personal and what is programmed, than the message, "Carmen, I love you," scrawled on the statue of a former president or under the ad for a transnational perfume?

We should be glad that monuments are being defied and revised by graffiti. We must rejoice that the city is not merely a pristine continuation of tidy spaces where historical landmarks are quietly integrated into contemporary life but, rather, a living organism capable of merging its past and present struggles. Although monuments often depict part of popular collective memory, albeit distorted or demagogically exalted by the authorities, they become more meaningful when resumed by the common man, when they are incorporated into the struggle for symbolic power and, consequently, into the contradictions of daily life.

The builders of monuments—artists and the government officials who commission them—can endow

In the swim of things. In front of a department store, an advertisement for a make of swimsuit (left); a pegasus in front of Bellas Artes, Alameda Park, Mexico City (right).

our cities with a new meaning if they do not restrict themselves to whitewashing the heroes and the values of the past, if they understand that their art can be much more than mere embellishments of the intersections and thoroughfares. As a vital aspect of public art in our cities teeming with freeways, expressways, neon signs, and high rises, monuments can give a new meaning to history, to the transformation of our sensitive and symbolic relations vis-à-vis the environment. Monuments should not glorify the city as the hub of power but, rather, should designate and recall its common meeting places and democratic exchanges. Perhaps someday more flexible shapes and new materials will enable them to express the social changes that emerge only amidst the fierce slogans painted on the walls. Why not have ephemeral, modifiable monuments built of wood, cloth, or paper, their surfaces free to be written on and erased, where the many forms of memory can join their aspirations? Not only would they tell us what has been experienced, but what is longing to be experienced.

Translator's Footnotes

1. José Borda (1699-1778) was a colorful half-French, half-Spanish adventurer who settled in early eighteenth-century Taxco, where he grew extremely wealthy by exploiting the silver mines in the region. He made and lost several fortunes in his lifetime due to his prodigal spending, but managed to leave his son, Dr. Manuel de la Borda, a considerable inheritance. One of Taxco's most popular hotels is named after him. Even now that the silver mines have seen better days, Taxco is still known far and wide for its exquisitely worked silver.

2. Carmen Serdán (1875-1948) and her brother, Aquiles Serdán, were staunch supporters of Francisco I. Madero during the Mexican Revolution of 1910, and were in charge of starting the revolt in their native Puebla. When the plot was discovered Aquiles lost his life, while his mother, wife, and sister, Carmen—who had been wounded—were imprisoned. When Madero finally rose to power Carmen was released and devoted herself to a nursing career.

3. Guillermo Prieto (1818-1897), poet, journalist, playwright, and politician, was born in Mexico City where he soon made his mark both as a prolific writer and as a Liberal party representative, senator, and finance minister during three presidential terms, including that of Benito Juárez.

4. The now famous towers of Ciudad Satélite were built in 1957 by architect Luis Barragán and sculptor-artist Mathias Goeritz. Each concrete tower is of a different height and is painted in a different color. The towers are located in the state of Mexico, north of Mexico City, and mark the entrance to Ciudad Satélite, now a burgeoning, upper-middle-class suburb of the nation's capital.

To the Sea Mine. This unexploded mine from the last world war was found in the harbor and placed on a pedestal in the penal colony of Islas Marias.

231   *Art for art's sake*. A marker in the middle of the fields on the way to Pachuca, Hidalgo, whose meaning no one could explain. It has been allowed to crumble away.

To sulphur, at the entrance to a sulphur mine near Minatitlán, Veracruz.

233   *To the fallen bastion*. A former governor of Campeche, a land speculator, razed most of the magnificent walls that defended Campeche City against the buccaneers. Now, on the outskirts, this fake bastion has been erected, a pathetic memento.

A spooky launch pad in Palmira, Cuernavaca, Morelos.

235   *A spiky sputnik* in Minatitlán, Veracruz, at the entrance to the oil refinery.

Pied pipes. A Monument to the Sewage System in San Martin Texmelucan, Puebla.

237   *Peep at the pipers*. A section of the deep sewage collector in Guadalajara, Jalisco, with the drilling drum that was turned into a monument by the addition of two bronze workers.

Where will you wander? A monument (as it says on the plaque) to the road-crossing, in the state of Veracruz.

RESPECTO DEL CAMINO QUE DE TEHUACAN CONDUCE A ESTA
CIUDAD . . . LA OBRA NO ES DIFICIL SI TENEMOS UNA VOLUNTAD
FIRME DE REALIZARLA EMPRENDAMOSLA Y TENDREMOS LA GLORIA
DE HABER H CHO UN BIEN POSITIVO A LOS PUEBLOS Y DEJARE-
OS A NUESTROS HIJOS UNA MEMORIA GRATA Y PERDURABLE.

CIUDAD DE OAXACA, 2 DE JULIO DE 1848
BENI O JUAREZ
GOB RNADOR DE ESTADO

239 *Wayside well-wisher*, near Telixtlahuaca, Oaxaca, on the fork of the road to Tehuacan.

Tapless tubes. The winner in a sculpture competition to use up steel pipes ordered for a gas pipeline that was not to be, in Monterrey.

240

241   *Tubeless taps.* This concrete water tap about twenty feet high tops a water tank on Cerro de los Remedios near Mexico City. Originally it had a recycled water flow for effect (and what an effect in this dry country!), but the pumping system has long since broken down.

Where e'er ye be . . . On all the major roads leading north, one will find a simplified globe to mark the Tropic of Cancer.

243   . . . *let the wind gae free* . . . As you come down the road that crosses the central desert of Baja California, straight as an arrow, you begin seeing an eagle-shaped thing wavering in the heat miles before you reach it. This huge project, to mark the 28th Parallel, includes a hotel, a school built underground that was never used, and this open-air auditorium.

. . . *was the death of me!* The towers of Ciudad Satélite near Mexico City (opposite and above) were the result of outstanding teamwork by Luis Barragán and Mathias Goeritz. Though now surrounded by dense construction, they still stand tall.

247   The availability of vast capital loans in the early eighties permitted extensive remodeling of urban centers. In Guadalajara a large section of the old town, from the Cathedral to the Hospicio Cabañas was demolished, and the huge Plaza Tapatía took its place, a large shopping center over a vast underground parking lot: the taxpayer foots the bill.

Mr. Eiffel . . . The tallest and slimmest urban sculpture in Mexico, Luis Barragán's bladelike tower was meant to be 100 meters high. Built in concrete, and painted shocking red, it's equipped with laser beams that signal the cardinal points of the city of Monterrey.

249   . . . *and Mr. Fell* (Humpty Dumpty?). Function is at the mercy of form in this auditorium in Tijuana, Baja California. A lot of official architecture, at the antipodes of discretion, takes over the attributes of the monument. This one is ostensibly derived from Alexandre Le Carré's visionary project of 1792.

251   *The Sculpture Space (Espacio Escultórico)* on the grounds of the National University of Mexico was designed in 1979 by a team of six sculptors. It is now one of the great sights of Mexico City. Neither monument or arena, it is a sculpted container of petrified lava, an homage to earth, man, and sky. Anonymous by intention, magical in spirit, it is nobody's in particular yet belongs to everyone.

INDEX